MW01245965

The Basketball Book for Kids

Everything Young Readers Need to Know About the Rules, History, Trivia, Best Teams and Biographies of the Greatest Players on the Court... It's More than Just a Game

Jasper Hall

Cover Photo by:

Dmytro Aksonov via

https://www.istockphoto.com/portfolio/Aksonov

Table of Contents

Chapter 1:
Introduction to the Game of Basketball

∞

Basketball is more than just a game; it's a dance of dexterity, a battle of balance, and a testament to teamwork. On courts in gyms, parks, and driveways, it's played by people from all walks of life, sharing a love for the excitement and spirit the game brings. To truly understand basketball, we must appreciate the skills it hones and the camaraderie it fosters.

Imagine you're watching a game – the court is a stage, the players are the performers, and the ball is the star of the show. As the players pivot, pass, and leap, each movement tells a story. Basketball teaches not only physical agility but mental acuity as well. It's a sport that asks you to think on your feet, predict your opponent's next move, and trust in your teammates' abilities.

The game is played on a rectangular court with a hoop at each end. The objective? To score points by getting the ball through the opponent's hoop. Sounds simple, right? But there's a catch – you can't just walk the ball to the basket, you have to bounce, or "dribble" it. And while you're trying to score, there's an opposing team equally determined to stop you and take the ball away. It's this back-and-forth, this electrifying exchange of offense and defense that hooks fans and players alike.

Let's not forget the rhythm of basketball. It's in the bounce of the ball, the squeak of sneakers on polished wood, and the beat of hearts racing in the final seconds of a close game. The game's pace can change in an instant – a slow, strategic set-up can explode into a fast break down the court, showcasing the players' speed and agility.

The spirit of the game lies in its values: respect, dedication, and teamwork. Players learn to respect themselves, their teammates, and their opponents. Dedication comes from hours of practice to master a free throw or to understand the nuances of a defensive strategy. And teamwork? It's the golden thread that ties everything together. No player can win the game alone; it takes a group working as one.

As you read through this book, remember that each dribble, each pass, and each shot is a building block of the game. Whether you're a fan cheering from the sidelines or a player pushing to improve, basketball has something to teach us all.

As our journey with the bouncing ball continues, let's explore the essence of what makes basketball truly special – the players. From the youngest child tossing a foam ball into a toy hoop to the professional athlete executing a perfect three-point shot in a stadium filled with thousands, basketball players share a bond that transcends age, language, and culture.

Picture this: a player crouches low, eyes fixed on the opponent, muscles coiled like a spring. The gym is silent, the air thick with anticipation. Then, in a flash, they leap, stealing the ball and racing toward the hoop. The crowd erupts as the ball swishes through the net, a perfect arc of triumph. This is the magic moment that captures hearts, the moment when skill meets opportunity, and a new fan is born.

Basketball isn't just about the individual moments of glory, though. It's about the day-in, day-out grind. It's about practicing until the sun sets, shooting free throws until the echo of the ball is your only companion in a quiet gym. It's about the push to be better than you were the day before, to support your teammates, and to share in the collective struggle and success.

It's also about the coaches who serve as guides, the unsung heroes shaping young minds and talents. They're the architects of the game, drawing up plays in huddles, instilling discipline, and inspiring passion. A good coach's influence extends beyond the court, teaching life lessons through the lens of sport.

And let's not forget the fans, the beating heart of basketball. In the stands, fans are a sea of faces, a chorus of voices, each with their own story of why they love this game. Some come for the thrill of competition, some for the sense of community, and others to witness athletic artistry in real time.

Basketball is also a language of its own, a universal dialect of dunks, dribbles, and dedication. It connects people across continents, whether it's a pickup game on a dirt court in a remote village or a championship game broadcast worldwide. It's a conversation between cultures, where the score is kept in points, but the real victories are in the friendships and understanding forged both on and off the court.

But remember, as much as basketball is about competition, it's also about community. It's about the shared experiences, the memories made, and the lessons learned. The game teaches resilience, how to cope with loss, and how to savor victory. Every player, coach, and fan knows that basketball, at its core, is about coming together, striving for a goal, and celebrating the human spirit.

Now that we've dribbled through the heartbeat of the game, let's bounce into the symphony of a basketball match. From the screeching sneakers and the steady dribble of the ball to the sharp whistle of the referee and the swoosh of the net, each sound combines to create the game's unique music.

In the vibrant atmosphere of a basketball game, every sense is engaged. The bright lights shine on the polished court, reflecting the swift movements of players in their colorful jerseys. The smell of the wooden floor, the leather ball, and the faint scent of popcorn from the stands fill the air, creating an ambiance that's distinctly 'basketball'.

Each game is a story with its own rhythm and pace. There are moments of tense stillness, like the calm before the storm, as a player prepares for a crucial free throw. The crowd holds its breath, the silence is palpable, and then there's the release—the shot—and the explosion of sound that follows, whether in joy or disappointment.

Basketball is a dance, where each player's movements are both independent and interdependent. Like a well-rehearsed chorus, they know when to come together for a defensive stand or to break away for an offensive play. There's a beauty in the coordination, in the unspoken understanding between teammates who have practiced and played together, who can anticipate each other's moves and create poetry in motion.

It's not just the physical aspects that make basketball enthralling. It's the mental game, too—the strategies discussed during timeouts, the split-second decisions made mid-play, the psychological warfare as players try to outwit and outlast their opponents. Each decision can turn the tide, each play can become a memorable moment.

And as the final buzzer sounds, win or lose, players shake hands. This gesture symbolizes respect and the shared passion for the game. The competition is fierce, but the camaraderie is fiercer. Players may battle for every point, but at the end of the day, they're part of a community that respects the game and each other.

We've only just scratched the surface of the rich tapestry that is basketball. In the upcoming chapters, we'll dive into the specific rules that guide the game, the history that shaped it, the skills needed to play it, and the cultures around the world that embrace it. We'll explore the lives of legendary players whose stories inspire us and learn how this game can teach us lessons far beyond scoring baskets.

Basketball is more than just a game. It's a journey, an education, a celebration of human potential. It's a world of its own, inviting you to jump in and be part of the magic. So lace up your sneakers, young reader, because the adventure is just beginning, and every page from here is another step in the grand dance of basketball.

Chapter 2:
The Rules of Basketball: Understanding the Game

Welcome to the core of basketball, the framework that holds our beloved game together: the rules. Knowing these rules doesn't just make the game fair—it makes it fun, challenging, and exciting. So, let's dribble down the court of knowledge and understand the guidelines that every player must follow, whether they are dreaming of professional play or just shooting hoops in the driveway.

The Basics: Object of the Game

Basketball is played by two teams, each with five players on the court at a time. The primary objective? Score points by shooting the basketball through the opponent's hoop from above while preventing the opposing team from doing so. Sounds simple, right? Well, there's more to it.

The Court

The playing field is a rectangular court with a hoop at each end. Lines marked on the court form its skeleton, defining boundaries and playing areas. The most prominent is the mid-court line, which splits the court into two equal halves. There are also the three-point arcs, free-throw lines, and the painted area known as the key or the lane.

Starting the Game

A game starts with a jump ball or tip-off. The referee throws the ball up between the two players in the center circle, and they leap to tip it to their teammates, signaling the beginning of a contest where every second counts.

Moving with the Ball

Once you have the ball, you can't just run with it. To move legally, you must dribble, bouncing the ball on the floor as you walk or run. If the ball stops bouncing, your feet must too, or else it's a travel violation. And watch out—dribble with both hands or double-dribble, and you'll hear the referee's whistle blow.

Scoring Points

Points are the currency of the game. A shot made from beyond the three-point line earns three points, while a basket scored from within this arc is worth two. Free throws, attempted from the free-throw line after certain fouls, are worth one point each.

The Shot Clock

Teams can't just hold onto the ball indefinitely; they have a limited time to attempt a shot. In professional leagues, the shot clock is typically 24 seconds. If the shot isn't off by then, the buzzer sounds, and the other team takes over.

Fouls and Violations

Fouls are the game's no-nos, actions that are too rough or illegal. Personal fouls involve unfair physical contact, which can send an opposing player to the free-throw line to shoot free throws. Technical fouls, on the other hand, can be called for unsportsmanlike conduct, and they give the opponents a free throw and possession of the ball.

Violations are different—they include traveling, double-dribbling, goal-tending (when a player interferes with a shot on its downward arc), and the shot clock running out. These result in the other team getting the ball.

Time-Outs

Both teams can call time-outs, brief breaks to discuss strategy or just catch their breath. It's a pause that can be both a moment of respite and a turning point in the game.

Substitutions

Tired players can be swapped out during breaks in play. Substitutions allow teams to bring fresh legs onto the court and to adjust their strategies.

This whirlwind tour of basketball rules is just the beginning. By knowing the rules, players can focus on the game's joy, the thrill of competition, and the satisfaction of skillful play. It's the solid groundwork upon which all the fun is built.

Let's lace up our sneakers and get ready to dive even deeper into the rule book. As we peel back the layers of the game, we start to see how each rule interlocks with the next, creating the intricate dance that is basketball.

Fouls Explained Further

Fouls can be a bit confusing, so let's break them down a little more. There are two main types of fouls: defensive and offensive. Defensive fouls happen when the defender makes illegal contact with the offensive player, like hitting their arm while they're shooting. Offensive fouls are the opposite, like when an offensive player charges into a defender who has established their position.

There's also something called a flagrant foul, which is when a player makes unnecessary or excessive contact against another player. This is a big no-no and can result in the offending player being ejected from the game.

Violations: A Closer Look

We've mentioned traveling and double dribbling, but there are a few more violations you should know about. One is the backcourt violation, which happens when the offensive team takes the ball back across the mid-court line after they've already brought it into the frontcourt. This isn't allowed because it would enable teams to waste time.

Another violation is the three-second rule. Offensive players can't stay within the key, the painted area near the basket, for more than three seconds at a time. This keeps the game moving and prevents players from camping out near the basket.

The Role of the Referees

Referees are the enforcers of the game, ensuring everyone plays by the rules. They call fouls and violations and are in charge of things like starting and stopping the game clock, inspecting the equipment, and deciding who gets the ball when it goes out of bounds. They need sharp eyes and a clear understanding of the rules to make split-second decisions.

Out of Bounds and Possession

If the ball or a player holding the ball touches the boundary lines, it's out of bounds. The opposing team is then given possession of the ball. This rule helps define the active play area and is crucial for setting up strategic plays.

The 8-Second Rule

Once the offensive team gains possession of the ball, they have 8 seconds to move the ball across the mid-court line into the frontcourt. This keeps the pace of the game fast and prevents stalling.

Over and Back

Remember the mid-court line we mentioned earlier? Once the ball has crossed this line into the offensive half, it cannot go back into the defensive half. If the offensive team does send the ball back, it's called an "over and back" violation, and the opposing team gets possession.

The 5-Second Rule

When a player is closely guarded and fails to pass, shoot, or dribble within five seconds, it's a violation. This rule encourages quick thinking and movement, keeping the game exciting.

By now, you're getting a sense of how dynamic and nuanced the rules of basketball are. They ensure the game is fair, safe, and enjoyable for everyone. But they're also designed to maintain a brisk and exhilarating pace of play.

In the next section, we will look at game strategies and how understanding the rules can give you an edge on the court. Stay tuned, because knowing the rules is just the beginning. Using them to your advantage? That's where the game gets really interesting.

Game Strategy and Rule Knowledge

Knowing the rules is one thing, but using them to your team's advantage is where the strategic aspect of basketball truly shines. For instance, understanding the shot clock—a timer designed to quicken the pace of the game by limiting the time a team can possess the ball before attempting a shot—can help teams create urgency and pressure the defense.

Shot Clock Savvy

In professional leagues like the NBA, the shot clock is typically set to 24 seconds, while in college basketball it might be longer. If a team doesn't attempt a shot that hits the rim within this time frame, they lose possession. Smart teams use the shot clock to their advantage by managing the clock to create scoring opportunities or limit the opponent's time with the ball.

Free Throws and the Bonus Situation

Free throws are awarded after certain fouls are committed. If a player is fouled while shooting, they get free throws—either two or three, depending on where the shot was taken from. Teams can also enter a "bonus" situation, where they get free throws after the opposing team commits a certain number of fouls within a period.

The Importance of Personal and Team Fouls

Each player is allowed a specific number of personal fouls per game (five in college and six in the NBA) before they're disqualified, or "fouled out," from the game. Teams must also be mindful of team fouls, as accumulating too many in a quarter or half can lead to bonus free throws for the opposition.

The Intricacies of Inbounding

When inbounding the ball, players have exactly five seconds to pass the ball onto the court to a teammate. Failure to do so results in a turnover. Teams often have special plays designed for inbounding the ball, especially in crucial moments of the game.

The Art of Substitution

Substitutions are a critical part of basketball strategy. Coaches must decide when to swap players to ensure the team remains fresh and competitive. There are rules governing substitutions, and they can only be made when play is stopped, and the referee acknowledges the request.

Timeouts: A Tactical Tool

Teams are allowed a certain number of timeouts during a game, which they can use to stop the clock, plan strategies, and make substitutions. Knowing when to call a timeout can change the momentum of the game or give the team a much-needed breather.

Jump Ball Situations

A game starts with a jump ball, and certain situations can lead to a jump ball during the game, such as when two players from opposing teams grab the ball simultaneously, and the referees cannot determine who has possession. Understanding how to position for and win a jump ball can be crucial, especially in close matches.

Last-Minute Strategies: The Role of the Clock

As the game clock winds down, especially in the last minutes, managing the clock becomes a vital strategy. Teams behind in the score may intentionally foul to stop the clock and regain possession after free throws, hoping the other team misses. On the other hand, teams ahead might use dribbling and passing to run down the clock.

Through this exploration of basketball rules, we've seen not just the framework that holds the game together, but also the strategic battleground that it creates. Mastery of these rules and the ability to leverage them in play is what separates good teams from the great ones. The discipline, quick decision-making, and tactical use of rules are as much a part of the game as the physical skills displayed on the court.

As you lace up your sneakers and step onto the court, carry with you not just the knowledge of how to dribble or shoot, but the understanding of the game's structure. It's this intricate ballet of rules and play that makes basketball the thrilling sport loved by millions around the globe.

Chapter 3:
The History of Basketball: From Peach Baskets to Professional Leagues

The game of basketball, as we know it today, was born out of necessity. In the winter of 1891, Dr. James Naismith, a physical education teacher at the International YMCA Training School in Springfield, Massachusetts, was challenged to create a game that could be played indoors during the cold winter months. With a soccer ball, two peach baskets nailed to the lower railing of the gymnasium balcony, and a set of 13 basic rules, Naismith invented a game that would become one of the world's most popular sports.

Naismith's game was simple: The ball had to be thrown into the peach baskets to score, and the team with the most baskets won. However, the baskets still had bottoms, so every time a shot went in, someone had to climb a ladder and retrieve the ball. It wasn't until a few years later that the bottoms were removed, allowing the ball to fall through.

The game quickly became popular among YMCA centers across the United States and Canada. It was seen not only as a fun activity but also as a way to promote a healthy lifestyle and foster teamwork among young men. By the early 1900s, basketball had spread to colleges, where the first formal games were played. It was in college gymnasiums that many of the game's early strategies and team plays were developed.

As basketball's popularity soared, the potential for a professional league became evident. The first professional league, the National Basketball League (NBL), was formed in 1898, but it didn't last long due to financial difficulties. It wasn't until 1946 that the Basketball Association of America (BAA), which would become the National Basketball Association (NBA) in 1949, was founded. This league would go on to become the premier professional basketball league in the world.

Over the years, basketball has evolved in both style of play and rules. The introduction of the three-point line, the shot clock, and various rule changes have shaped the modern game. Players have become bigger, faster, and stronger, and the level of athleticism displayed in contemporary basketball is at an all-time high.

Throughout its history, basketball has been influenced by iconic players who have transcended the sport. Figures like George Mikan, the first dominant "big man"; Bill Russell, with his unmatched defensive prowess; Wilt Chamberlain, who scored 100 points in a single game; Magic Johnson and Larry Bird, whose rivalry captured the imagination of fans; and Michael Jordan, arguably the greatest of all time, have each left an indelible mark on basketball.

What started as a simple game in a small gym in Massachusetts has become a global phenomenon. The formation of the International Basketball Federation (FIBA) in 1932, and basketball's inclusion in the 1936 Berlin Olympics, signaled the sport's international reach. Today, the NBA boasts a host of international players, and basketball leagues around the world are thriving.

This section of Chapter 3 has traced the origins and early expansion of basketball from a simple school game to a global professional sport. Next, we will delve deeper into the milestones and major events that have shaped the game's history and explore the legendary teams and moments that have defined generations.

As the 20th century progressed, basketball witnessed several key milestones that helped shape the sport into what it is today.

In 1949, two rival leagues, the Basketball Association of America (BAA) and the National Basketball League (NBL), merged to form the National Basketball Association (NBA). This unification brought together the best talents and set the stage for a more organized and competitive professional basketball scene.

College basketball began to take center stage, especially with the NCAA Men's Basketball Tournament, also known as "March Madness." Started in 1939, this annual competition has grown into a highly anticipated event, drawing millions of fans and creating legends through buzzer-beaters and Cinderella stories.

The mid-20th century also marked important strides in social progress within basketball. In 1950, Earl Lloyd became the first African American to play in an NBA game, paving the way for the integration of the league. This was a significant step toward racial equality in American sports.

The latter part of the 20th century saw basketball's popularity surge globally. Key moments that facilitated this include:

The Olympics

The inclusion of basketball in the 1936 Olympics in Berlin was a critical moment for the international growth of the sport. It was an opportunity for countries to showcase their talents on a world stage, and the sport quickly became a staple of the Olympic Games.

FIBA's Influence

The International Basketball Federation (FIBA) played a significant role in spreading the game worldwide. The first FIBA Basketball World Cup was held in 1950, furthering the sport's international reach and promoting global competition.

The Dream Team

The 1992 Barcelona Olympics featured the "Dream Team" from the United States, composed of NBA stars like Michael Jordan, Magic Johnson, and Larry Bird. Their participation not only captivated audiences worldwide but also inspired a new generation of players outside the U.S.

Women's Basketball

The Women's National Basketball Association (WNBA) was founded in 1996 as a counterpart to the NBA. It provided a platform for female athletes to showcase their talent at a professional level.

The USA Women's National Team has been a dominant force in the Olympics and World Championships, further promoting the sport among female athletes and contributing to its popularity.

The Cultural Impact

The style and attire associated with basketball, like sneakers and jerseys, have become global fashion statements, thanks in part to player endorsements and the blending of sports with hip-hop culture.

Films, video games, and literature centered around basketball have become part of the cultural fabric, creating a multimedia ecosystem that surrounds and enhances the sport.

As we've explored in this segment, basketball's evolution has been shaped by pivotal events, social progress, global expansion, the empowerment of women, and cultural integration. In the following sections, we will take a closer look at the legendary teams, games, and moments that have solidified basketball's place in the annals of sports history.

As basketball evolved, certain teams rose to prominence, their legacies etched into the very fabric of the game. These teams not only dominated the sport during their prime but also helped to elevate the popularity of basketball globally.

The Celtics Dynasty

The Boston Celtics, under the tutelage of coach Red Auerbach and led by Bill Russell, became the emblem of excellence and teamwork in the 1950s and 1960s. They won an unprecedented 11 championships in 13 seasons, including eight in a row from 1959 to 1966. The Celtics' emphasis on collective play over individual stardom set the standard for future generations.

The Showtime Lakers

In the 1980s, the Los Angeles Lakers, known for their "Showtime" brand of basketball, captured the hearts of fans. With Magic Johnson at the helm, the Lakers' fast-paced, flashy style and their rivalry with the Celtics, who had found a new star in Larry Bird, brought an unmatched excitement to the NBA.

The Chicago Bulls' Three-Peats

The Chicago Bulls, led by Michael Jordan, created a global phenomenon in the 1990s. Their two three-peats (winning three championships in a row) in 1991-93 and 1996-98 were pivotal, showcasing not just athletic prowess but also the mental and strategic aspects of the game.

On the women's side, the game has been equally impacted by outstanding teams that have demonstrated excellence and pushed the sport forward.

The Tennessee Lady Vols

Under the guidance of Pat Summitt, the University of Tennessee's Lady Vols became a powerhouse in women's college basketball. Their success helped elevate the women's game to new heights and inspired countless young girls to pursue the sport.

The Houston Comets' Reign

The Houston Comets dominated the WNBA in its formative years, winning the first four championships of the league from 1997 to 2000. They set a high bar for excellence in professional women's basketball and contributed to the league's stability and growth.

In tandem with the rise of these legendary teams, basketball continued to solidify its status internationally.

European basketball grew stronger, with teams like Spain's FC Barcelona and Russia's CSKA Moscow consistently performing at a high level in the EuroLeague. Their success has been critical in developing local talents who would go on to have significant careers in the NBA and international competitions.

Countries like China and the Philippines embraced basketball with fervor, while in Africa, the sport has become a beacon of hope and a pathway to a better life for many young talents. The establishment of the Basketball Africa League (BAL) in 2020 is a testament to the sport's growth on the continent.

Basketball's history is more than just a record of who won or lost; it's a chronicle of social change, community building, and the breaking down of barriers. As the NBA, WNBA, and other leagues around the world continue to innovate and expand, they carry with them the legacy of the teams and players that laid the foundation for today's global basketball community.

From peach baskets to the bright lights of modern arenas, basketball's journey reflects a sport that has continuously adapted and thrived. Its history is a vibrant tapestry, rich with stories of triumph, unity, and the relentless pursuit of excellence.

Chapter 4:
How to Play Basketball: Skills and Drills for Beginners

Basketball is an exciting game that combines athleticism, strategy, and skill. To play basketball, you need to know the basics—how to dribble, shoot, pass, and play defense. This chapter will take you through the fundamental skills of basketball and provide drills that can help you become a better player. Remember, practice makes perfect, so grab your ball, and let's get started!

Getting Started: Warm-Up

Before you jump into playing, it's important to warm up. A good warm-up prepares your body for the activities ahead and helps prevent injuries.

Warm-Up Drills

Jogging: Start with a light jog around the court. This gets your muscles warmed up and ready for more strenuous activity.

Stretching: Stretch your arms, legs, and back. Hold each stretch for at least 15 seconds. Don't bounce or push yourself too hard.

Jump Rope: This is great for footwork and conditioning. Try to jump rope for a few minutes to get your heart rate up.

Dribbling: Controlling the Ball

Dribbling is one of the most important skills in basketball. It's how you move the ball around the court without walking or running with it. Being able to handle the ball with confidence is crucial. It allows you to navigate through defenders and maintain possession under pressure.

Dribbling Drills

Stationary Dribbling: Stand in place and dribble the ball with your right hand for 30 seconds, then switch to your left hand. Keep your head up so you can see the court.

Cone Dribble: Set up cones (or any markers) in a line and dribble the ball in and out of the cones as quickly as you can while maintaining control.

Speed Dribble: Dribble as fast as you can from one end of the court to the other. Focus on pushing the ball forward and running after it rather than slapping it.

Figure-Eight Dribbling: Dribble the ball in a figure-eight pattern around and between your legs. This helps improve your hand-eye coordination and ball control.

Two-Ball Dribbling: Dribble two balls at once to improve your ambidexterity. It's tricky at first, but it's great for developing equal skill in both hands.

Behind the Back Dribble: Practice dribbling behind your back to protect the ball from defenders.

Crossover Dribble: Work on changing direction quickly with a sharp crossover dribble.

Spin Move: A spin move can help you evade a defender and change direction rapidly.

Shooting: Scoring Points

Shooting is how you score points in basketball. There are many different types of shots, but let's start with the most basic—the layup and the jump shot.

Layups: Practice layups from both the left and right sides of the basket. Focus on using the backboard.

Free Throws: Stand at the free-throw line and practice your shot. Remember to use your legs for power and follow through with your arm.

Jump Shots: Start close to the basket and work your way out. Get into a rhythm—dribble, stop, and shoot.

Good shooting form is essential. The BEEF principle can help you remember the basics: Balance, Eyes, Elbow, Follow-through.

Shooting Technique Drills

Form Shooting: Practice shooting close to the hoop to focus on your form without the pressure of distance.

Spot Shooting: Shoot from various spots around the court to work on your range and accuracy.

Shooting on the Move: Practice shooting after dribbling or running to simulate game situations.

Free Throws: Practice your free throws daily. Consistency here can be a game-changer during close matches.

Jump Shot: Work on your jump shot from different spots on the court. Focus on form and follow-through.

Three-Pointers: Once you're comfortable with mid-range shots, extend your range to three-pointers.

Find Your Rhythm: Everyone has a natural shooting rhythm; find yours and practice it.

Balance is Key: Work on getting your legs under you for balance in your shot, no matter where you are on the court.

Follow Through: Always follow through with your wrist, pointing your shooting hand in the direction of the basket.

Passing: Sharing the Ball

Passing is crucial in basketball. Good passing can get the ball to an open player, create scoring opportunities, and help avoid turnovers.

Passing Drills

Partner Passing: Find a partner and practice chest passes, bounce passes, and overhead passes. Aim for the chest area.

Wall Passing: If you don't have a partner, use a wall. Pass the ball against the wall, using different types of passes.

Passing Relay: Set up a small course with cones, and dribble to each cone before passing the ball to your partner.

Chest Pass: Practice pushing the ball from your chest to a partner with two hands for a precise pass.

Bounce Pass: Work on bouncing the ball to your partner, aiming for it to arrive waist high.

Overhead Pass: Use an overhead pass to get the ball to a teammate over a defender.

Defense: Stopping the Opponent

Defense is just as important as offense. Being a good defender can prevent the other team from scoring and smart defense is about anticipation and understanding the opponent's strategy. Controlling the rebounds can often be the difference between winning and losing.

Defensive Drills

Defensive Slides: Slide from one side of the paint to the other. Stay low, with your feet apart and your hands up.

Closeout Drills: Practice running toward a spot and then breaking down into a defensive stance as if you're guarding an opponent.

Rebounding Drills: Practice jumping and grabbing the ball off the backboard or rim.

Box Out Drills: Practice positioning your body between the opponent and the basket to secure the rebound.

Jumping Drills: Work on your vertical leap, which is crucial for rebounding.

Mirror Drill: Pair up with another player and try to copy their movements as they dribble the ball. This helps improve your reaction time.

Defensive Recovery: Have a coach or another player simulate a pass to an offensive player, and practice closing the gap quickly and getting into defensive position.

Teamwork: Playing with Others

Basketball is a team sport. Playing well with others involves communication, understanding your role, and being aware of your teammates and opponents.

Teamwork Drills

3-on-2 Drills: Have three players on offense and two on defense. This drill helps you work on passing and moving without the ball.

Scrimmage: Playing a scrimmage game is one of the best ways to practice teamwork. It gives you a real-game feel and helps you understand how to apply all the skills you've learned.

Give and Go: This is a basic offensive play where you pass to a teammate and immediately move towards the basket for a return pass.

Pick and Roll: A pick and roll involve setting a screen (the pick) for a teammate with the ball and then moving toward the basket (the roll) to receive a pass.

Defensive Teamwork: Practice team defense drills where communication, switching on screens, and helping out are key components.

Team Communication

Communication on the court is key to a well-functioning team. This includes both verbal and non-verbal cues. Always communicate with your teammates on the court.

Communication Drills

Call for the Ball: When playing a scrimmage or practice game, make sure to call out when you're open. This helps develop vocal presence on the court.

Defense Communication: Practice calling out screens and switches on defense, so your teammates know what to expect.

Understand Your Role: Know your role on the team and play to your strengths.

Trust Your Teammates: Trust is a big part of team dynamics; trust your teammates and they will trust you back.

Remember, every time you step onto the court, you have a chance to get better. Use these drills to work on your skills, and don't forget to cool down and stretch after your practice to keep your muscles in good shape.

Understanding the Positions

There are five main positions in basketball: point guard, shooting guard, small forward, power forward, and center. Each position has a specific role to play on the court.

Point Guard: Often the team leader and playmaker, responsible for directing plays.

Shooting Guard: Generally the team's best shooter and often responsible for scoring points.

Small Forward: Versatile players who can both score and defend.

Power Forward: Strong players who can dominate in rebounding and close-range shots.

Center: Typically the tallest player, who plays near the basket to block shots and get rebounds.

Position-Specific Drills

Guard Drills: Practice handling the ball, making quick decisions, and accurate passing.

Forward Drills: Work on agility and shooting from mid-range. Forwards should also practice post moves and rebounding.

Center Drills: Focus on strength and post moves close to the basket, as well as blocking shots and rebounding.

Taking Care of Your Body

Basketball is a physically demanding sport. Taking care of your body through proper nutrition, hydration, and rest is important to maintain your performance and avoid injuries.

Body Care Tips

Hydration: Drink plenty of water before, during, and after playing.

Nutrition: Eat a balanced diet with enough carbohydrates for energy and protein for muscle repair.

Sleep: Get enough rest so your body can recover from the physical demands of the sport.

Developing as a basketball player involves building a consistent practice routine that covers all aspects of the game. Use the drills and tips in this chapter to create a practice schedule that works for you. Remember to focus on your weaknesses, but also play to your strengths.

Developing Court Vision

Having good court vision means being aware of everything happening on the court and making smart decisions.

Court Vision Drills

Peripheral Vision: Try to focus on a point while being aware of the movement around you to improve your peripheral vision.

Scrimmage: In-game practice is one of the best ways to develop court vision.

Conditioning

To play basketball well, you need to be in top physical condition.

Conditioning Drills

Sprints: Improve your speed and endurance with sprinting drills.

Agility Ladder: Use an agility ladder to improve your foot speed and coordination.

Mental Toughness

The mental aspect of basketball is just as important as the physical. The difference between good players and great ones often lies in their mental approach.

Mental Toughness Drills

Visualization: Spend time visualizing successful plays and what you want to achieve on the court.

Pressure Situations: Practice free throws or other drills while tired or with distractions to simulate pressure situations.

Concentration Exercises: Improve your focus by doing drills that require high concentration, like dribbling through cones while keeping your head up.

Positive Self-Talk: Practice positive self-talk to build confidence and stay motivated during practice and games.

Game Simulation: Mimic game situations in practice to prepare mentally for real-game pressure.

Practice Games

Finally, putting all your skills to the test in practice games is vital. They can help you understand how the pieces of basketball skills fit together in a real game setting.

Practice Game Tips

Pick-Up Games: Engage in pick-up games that can offer real-time situations and varied playing styles.

Mini-Games: Create scenarios with specific objectives, like playing defense without fouling or only scoring with layups.

By mastering these skills and drills and continually practicing them, you'll develop into a well-rounded basketball player. Remember, the key to improvement is not just in understanding these concepts but also in applying them consistently in practice and games. Stay dedicated, and watch as your skills, confidence, and love for the game grow.

Basketball is not just about the physical skills but also the bonds you create with teammates, the memories you make on the court, and the life lessons it teaches you about perseverance, teamwork, and the joy of playing the game. Keep pushing yourself, remain patient, and enjoy the journey of improving your game!

.

Chapter 5:
Leagues and Conferences: Exploring Professional and Amateur Basketball

Basketball is not just a game; it's a vast ecosystem that encompasses various leagues and conferences, each with its own story, structure, and significance. Whether it's a child shooting hoops with dreams of making it big or a professional athlete playing in a packed arena, these structured competitions provide a stage for every player. In this chapter, we will delve into the details of professional and amateur basketball, understanding what makes each league and conference unique and vital to the sport's global narrative.

Professional Basketball Leagues

The National Basketball Association (NBA)

The NBA is the zenith of basketball leagues, a North American professional basketball juggernaut with a global following. Its structure is meticulously crafted, with two conferences: the Eastern and Western. Each conference is further divided into three divisions, with teams battling through an 82-game regular season to secure a spot in the playoffs. The playoffs are a high-stakes, knockout format culminating in the NBA Finals, where two teams compete for the championship title.

The NBA is a brand as much as it is a league, known for its high-flying dunks, star athletes, and multi-million dollar contracts. It's an aspirational summit for any basketball player and a benchmark for basketball excellence worldwide.

NBA G League

The G League, formerly known as the NBA Development League or D-League, functions as the NBA's farming ground, offering a platform for players to develop their skills and gain the experience necessary to play at the highest level. It's a mix of young talent fresh from the draft, seasoned professionals looking to reinvigorate their careers, and international players seeking exposure in the American basketball scene. The G League is a testament to the NBA's commitment to developing basketball talent and expanding the sport's reach.

International Leagues

The passion for basketball spills over borders, with professional leagues in Europe, Asia, and beyond showcasing regional flavors of the game.

EuroLeague

Considered the premier professional basketball club competition in Europe, the EuroLeague brings together elite teams from different European national leagues. Modeled somewhat after soccer's UEFA Champions League, it represents the pinnacle of European club basketball. The talent pool is rich, with many players having either NBA experience or aspirations, making it a fertile ground for scouting by NBA teams.

Other Leagues

Around the globe, other professional leagues make their mark. Latin America, Asia, and Oceania all have thriving basketball ecosystems, with the likes of the Argentinian LNB, the Chinese CBA, and the Australian NBL. Each league contributes to the sport in its unique way, providing a stage for local talent and helping to grow the game globally.

Women's Basketball Leagues

Women's National Basketball Association (WNBA)

The WNBA stands as the counterpart to the NBA for female athletes in the U.S., showcasing the highest level of women's basketball in the world. Its players are among the best, often participating in international leagues during the WNBA offseason. The WNBA has been pivotal in highlighting women's sports, advocating for gender equality in athletics, and inspiring countless young girls to play basketball.

37

International Women's Leagues

Internationally, women's professional basketball leagues also exhibit high levels of play and competition. The EuroLeague Women, analogous to the men's EuroLeague, features top European clubs. The Women's Korean Basketball League (WKBL) and the Women's Chinese Basketball Association (WCBA) are also prominent, with their own sets of stars and competitive seasons. These leagues are critical in promoting women's basketball, offering professional opportunities for female athletes worldwide.

Amateur Basketball

College Basketball

The NCAA oversees college basketball in the U.S., where young talent is nurtured and showcased. College basketball holds a special place in the American sports landscape, with institutions like Duke, Kentucky, and North Carolina being almost as well-known as some professional teams. The NCAA tournament, famously known as March Madness, is a cultural phenomenon that captures the nation's attention every spring.

High School Basketball

High school basketball is the first serious level of organized basketball for many players. It's where fundamental skills are polished and where players begin to make a name for themselves. High school tournaments and championships often draw considerable local attention, and for some players, they serve as a launchpad to collegiate, if not professional, careers.

Youth and Recreational Leagues

At the grassroots level, youth and recreational leagues play a crucial role in introducing the game to new players. They are vital for community engagement, promoting physical fitness, and teaching the values of teamwork and fair play. These leagues are the foundation of basketball's future, ensuring that the sport continues to thrive at the local level.

International Competitions

FIBA World Cup

Held every four years, the FIBA Basketball World Cup is the premier international basketball tournament for men's national teams. It's a showcase of the world's basketball prowess, featuring a blend of NBA stars and the best international talents. It's an opportunity for countries to shine on the global stage and for lesser-known players to emerge as international stars.

Olympic Basketball

Basketball became an official Olympic sport in 1936, and since then, it has been one of the highlights of the Summer Games. The Olympics are not just about winning; they symbolize international peace and unity through sport. For basketball players, it's an honor to represent their country and strive for Olympic gold.

Development Programs and Junior Leagues

NBA and WNBA Junior Programs

The NBA and WNBA have also been instrumental in fostering young talent through junior programs, which include camps, clinics, and youth leagues. These initiatives are aimed at developing fundamental basketball skills, understanding of the game, and promoting a healthy and active lifestyle among children and teenagers.

FIBA's Youth Tournaments

FIBA organizes youth tournaments such as the FIBA U19 Basketball World Cup and the FIBA U17 Basketball World Cup. These tournaments are critical for spotting future stars and providing them with early exposure to international competition.

Collegiate and Amateur League Influence

The NCAA's Role in Player Development

The NCAA plays a pivotal role in developing players for professional leagues, particularly the NBA and WNBA. For many players, college basketball is a stepping stone to the professional arena. It's here that they hone their skills, gain significant exposure through televised games and national championships, and learn to balance athletics with academics.

International Presence in College Basketball

The influence of international players in NCAA basketball has grown, with many young athletes from around the world choosing to play for American colleges. This not only elevates the level of competition but also adds a diverse flair to the styles of play seen across conferences.

The Cultural Impact of Basketball Leagues

From the NBA's global outreach to the universal appeal of FIBA's World Cup, basketball speaks a global language that transcends borders. The sport has become a medium for international diplomacy and cultural exchange. Players often become ambassadors of goodwill, promoting peace and understanding through basketball.

Professional and amateur basketball leagues significantly contribute to local and national economies through job creation, tourism, and infrastructure development. They also play a crucial role in social development by offering programs that support education, health, and leadership among youths.

Leagues and conferences face challenges like economic disparities, maintaining competitive balance, and dealing with social issues within and outside the sports community. How these organizations address these challenges will shape the future of the sport.

Technology is revolutionizing how leagues operate, from the use of analytics in scouting and game strategies to enhancing fan engagement through social media and streaming services. Embracing these changes is vital for leagues to stay relevant and competitive.

The expansion and increased visibility of women's basketball remain a priority. Greater investment and media coverage are essential for the growth of women's leagues. Success stories like the WNBA are inspiring, but much work remains to elevate women's basketball worldwide.

Basketball leagues and conferences are more than just organizers of sport; they are institutions that reflect and influence society. They are the heartbeat of the basketball community, providing opportunities for players and enjoyment for fans. The future of basketball lies in the continued evolution and collaboration of these leagues, fostering the sport from the grassroots to the global stage, ensuring its place not just as a pastime but as a vital part of our cultural fabric.

As we look forward, the narrative of basketball will be written by the successes and challenges of these leagues and conferences. It's a story that continues to unfold, inviting each new generation to be a part of this exhilarating journey on and off the court.

Chapter 6:
Teams to Know: Famous Basketball Clubs and Their Histories

When we talk about basketball, the teams are the beating heart of the game's rich history. They're the cradles of competition, the homes of heroes, and the birthplaces of the moments we never forget. This chapter is a journey through time and across courts, from the hallowed hardwoods of storied franchises to the modern marvels of the game's greatest gatherings.

Basketball's inception as a structured sport came at a time when America was in the throes of the Industrial Revolution. The game's early adaptation from a simple gym activity to a structured competitive endeavor reflected the society's growing appetite for organized sports. Following Dr. James Naismith's invention of the game in 1891, basketball quickly caught the public's imagination. The simplicity of its rules and the minimal equipment required made it accessible to many.

The Trenton Nationals were more than just the first professional basketball team; they were trailblazers in a sport that was yet to find its professional identity. Established in 1896 in New Jersey, the Nationals were among the pioneers of the professional game, moving basketball beyond a recreational pastime to a serious athletic competition. Their creation signaled the sport's potential for professional play and set a standard for the organized basketball that would follow.

Following the Nationals, a flurry of teams began to form. Each had a unique origin story, often tied to the local communities or the visionary entrepreneurs of the time. Teams like the New York Wanderers, the Bristol Pile Drivers, and the Camden Electrics didn't just represent their cities or companies; they were embodiments of the communities' spirit and pride. These teams played in makeshift courts, with varying levels of organization, but their passion for the game was a constant that drew crowds and built the foundations of the fan culture we see today.

The early basketball clubs operated independently at first, arranging matches amongst themselves, which laid the groundwork for the establishment of formal leagues. As these clubs grew in number, the need for organized competition became apparent. It wasn't long before regional leagues began to form, providing a structured environment for these teams to compete, and offering spectators a consistent schedule of games to enjoy.

In this nascent stage of club basketball, the equipment and players' attire were far from what we are accustomed to today. Early basketballs were inconsistent in shape and bounce, and the hoops were literal peach baskets affixed to the walls of gyms. The players wore rudimentary uniforms that were more akin to casual work attire than the athletic gear of modern players. Yet, these limitations did not deter the athletes or the fans. The spirit of competition and community engagement was vibrant, overshadowing the sport's humble material beginnings.

The significance of these early basketball clubs cannot be overstated. They provided a template for the professional teams that would come later. Their games helped refine the rules of basketball, transitioning from Dr. Naismith's original thirteen rules to a more complex set that would govern professional play. They also played a crucial role in popularizing the sport, demonstrating its viability as a spectator event, and its potential to grow beyond the YMCA gyms where it was first played.

Many of the original clubs are no longer active, or their lineages have morphed into modern teams, but their legacy is enduring. The Trenton Nationals, the New York Wanderers, the Bristol Pile Drivers, and the Camden Electrics, among others, laid the hardwood for the professional basketball landscape we see today. They showed that basketball could be more than just a game; it could be a profession, a passion, and a way of bringing communities together.

Through the lens of these early clubs, we can appreciate the transformation of basketball from its humble beginnings to the professional, polished sport that captivates millions worldwide. Their stories are foundational chapters in the grand narrative of basketball history.

The Original Celtics: Forging the Future of Professional Basketball

In the landscape of early professional basketball, the Original Celtics stand as titans, their impact rippling through time. Their origin story begins in the bustling streets of New York City, where the team was formed in 1915. However, it was in the 1920s that they etched their name in history. They were 'original' not just by name but in their innovative approach to the game, which would influence basketball in countless ways.

The Celtics revolutionized basketball with their sophisticated team play and defensive tactics. They introduced set plays and a series of coordinated movements that were unprecedented in the relatively free-form play of the time. Their style was a precursor to the systematic strategies employed by today's professional teams.

The team's grueling schedule was unheard of at the time. Playing more than 150 games a year, the Celtics traveled across the United States, earning them the nickname "barnstormers." They would challenge local teams, entertain crowds with their exceptional skills, and promote the professional game. Their endurance and dedication to the sport were instrumental in showcasing basketball's potential as a professional sport with a national appeal.

The Original Celtics were more than a basketball team; they were cultural icons of the 1920s. They brought basketball to rural areas and big cities alike, often being the first introduction to organized basketball for many spectators. Their flair on the court and their ability to draw crowds made them one of the most successful teams of their era both in terms of victories and financial success.

The players were larger-than-life characters, with the likes of Joe Lapchick, Johnny Beckman, and Nat Holman – who would later become one of basketball's most influential coaches – leading the charge. They became early examples of basketball celebrities, with playing styles that would inspire the next generation of players.

The tactics and techniques introduced by the Original Celtics laid the foundation for modern basketball. Their team-centric approach, focus on defense, and innovative plays were adopted by other teams and eventually became standard practice in the sport. The barnstorming model they popularized also paved the way for the establishment of national leagues, demonstrating that there was a viable audience for basketball across the country.

While the Original Celtics disbanded in the late 1930s, their influence did not wane. Many of the players went on to coach and stayed involved in basketball, spreading the Celtics' philosophy and contributing to the development of the sport. The team's legacy was formally recognized when they were inducted as a unit into the Basketball Hall of Fame, a testament to their role as pioneers of professional basketball.

The story of the Original Celtics is a testament to the passion and innovation that drove the early days of professional basketball. They showcased an unprecedented dedication to the sport, traversed uncharted territories in athletics, and left an indelible mark on basketball history. Through their travels, they spread the popularity of basketball, setting the stage for what would become one of the world's most beloved sports.

Boston Celtics: A Legacy of Champions

When the Boston Celtics were established in 1946 as part of the Basketball Association of America (BAA), which later became the NBA, the sports landscape of Boston was forever changed. The team's name, chosen for its connections to Boston's Irish population and history, resonated with the city's community and promised a deep-rooted cultural tie.

The Celtics' journey to becoming a basketball dynasty did not begin with immediate success. Like many fledgling teams, they faced challenges on the court, struggling to find their rhythm in the competitive arena of professional basketball. Yet, their perseverance would eventually pay off, setting the stage for an era of unprecedented success.

The turning point for the Celtics came with the hiring of Arnold "Red" Auerbach as coach in 1950. Auerbach was a visionary who would revolutionize the game with his emphasis on team play and a fast-break offense. His coaching philosophy centered around the concept of the "Celtics way"—a selfless style of basketball that valued the team above any individual.

In 1956, the Celtics made a pivotal decision by drafting center Bill Russell, who would become the cornerstone of the team's defense. Russell's arrival marked the beginning of a dominant period for the

Celtics, as his shot-blocking and rebounding prowess changed the way defense was played in the NBA.

The Celtics' dominance in the 1960s remains one of the most remarkable achievements in professional sports. Under Auerbach's leadership and Russell's on-court dominance, the Celtics won 11 championships in 13 years, including an incredible eight consecutive titles from 1959 to 1966. This period also featured legendary players like John Havlicek, Bob Cousy, and Sam Jones.

The Celtics' success was not limited to their championship titles. They were pioneers in breaking down racial barriers in the league. Red Auerbach made history by drafting Chuck Cooper in 1950, the first African American player drafted into the NBA. Later, by appointing Bill Russell as the first African American NBA coach in 1966, the Celtics continued to lead the way toward progress.

The Boston Celtics' legacy is marked by several eras of success, including the notable achievements of the 1980s team led by Larry Bird. Bird, along with Kevin McHale and Robert Parish, constituted the Celtics' frontline that brought home three additional championships in 1981, 1984, and 1986. Their rivalry with the Los Angeles Lakers, particularly with Magic Johnson, added a storied chapter to NBA history.

In the new millennium, the Celtics continue to be a beacon of excellence. The 2008 championship, led by Paul Pierce, Kevin Garnett, and Ray Allen, marked the franchise's 17th title, solidifying their status as the most decorated franchise in NBA history. The team's unwavering commitment to excellence and the cultivation of talent continue to be the hallmark of the Boston Celtics' enduring legacy.

As storied as their past, the Boston Celtics' narrative is one of resilience, innovation, and unyielding spirit. Their 17 championships are not just a tally of victories but a chronicle of basketball evolution and the relentless pursuit of greatness that has inspired countless athletes and fans around the globe. Through decades of change, the Boston Celtics' legacy remains an integral chapter in the annals of basketball history, representing a legacy of champions that transcends the sport itself.

Los Angeles Lakers: The Showtime Dynasty

Before the bright lights of Los Angeles, the Lakers were Minneapolis's pride, named after the state of Minnesota's moniker, "Land of 10,000 Lakes." The Lakers' early years were defined by the dominance of George Mikan, the NBA's first superstar. The team's success in Minneapolis laid the groundwork for its future glories, winning five championships before their relocation to Los Angeles in 1960.

The move to Los Angeles was a pivotal moment for the Lakers. It was not just a change in location but a transformation in identity. In Los Angeles, the Lakers would grow to become one of the most glamorous and successful franchises in sports history. The city's glitz and glamour became synonymous with the Lakers' brand, attracting a star-studded audience to their games.

The 'Showtime' Lakers, a name coined in the 1980s, turned basketball games into entertainment spectacles. With the drafting of Earvin "Magic" Johnson in 1979, the Lakers found the perfect leader for their fast-paced and exhilarating style of play. Magic's exceptional height for a point guard, coupled with his extraordinary passing abilities, allowed the Lakers to play an up-tempo game with a level of showmanship that had never been seen before in the NBA.

Behind the glitz and the fast breaks was the strategic mind of head coach Pat Riley. Taking the reins in the early '80s, Riley crafted an offense that leveraged Magic Johnson's unique skill set and emphasized speed, spacing, and passing. His vision cemented the Lakers as the team of the decade and became the face of an era in basketball that would never be forgotten.

The Showtime Lakers were more than just Magic Johnson. They featured an array of stars including Kareem Abdul-Jabbar, whose patented skyhook became one of the most unstoppable moves in basketball history, and James Worthy, whose nickname "Big Game James" was a testament to his playoff performances. Players like Byron Scott, Michael Cooper, and A.C. Green played crucial roles, while the Lakers' bench was deep with contributors who could step up at any moment.

The Showtime Lakers are perhaps best remembered for their fierce rivalry with the Boston Celtics. The Lakers and Celtics met several times in the NBA Finals during the '80s, with their contrasting styles and coasts adding fuel to the fire. This rivalry was headlined by the personal and professional competition between Magic Johnson and

Larry Bird, which began in college and blossomed into one of the greatest individual rivalries in sports history.

The Showtime Lakers won five NBA championships during the '80s (1980, 1982, 1985, 1987, and 1988), leaving an indelible mark on the NBA. Their impact on the game went beyond victories and titles; they played a key role in popularizing the NBA globally. The style, charisma, and success of the Showtime Lakers elevated basketball to new heights and set the standard for what an entertainment and sports hybrid could look like.

Today, the Los Angeles Lakers continue to build upon the legacy of the Showtime era. With stars like Kobe Bryant, who brought five more championships in the 2000s and 2010s, and LeBron James, continuing to push the franchise's success into the new millennium, the Lakers' tradition of excellence and their commitment to an exciting brand of basketball endure.

The Showtime era may have passed, but it forever changed the landscape of the NBA, leaving behind memories of a dynasty that dazzled and delighted, redefining what it means to be champions in the world of sports. The Los Angeles Lakers' Showtime dynasty, with its fusion of sports excellence and Hollywood flair, remains one of the most iconic and beloved chapters in the history of basketball.

Chicago Bulls: The Jordan Era

The Chicago Bulls, established in 1966, had experienced success but were not considered a basketball powerhouse until the arrival of Michael Jordan in 1984. Jordan's entry into the NBA heralded a new era not only for the Bulls but for the league as a whole. He brought an electrifying presence to the court that reinvigorated the team and ignited the fanbase.

It wasn't until the late '80s and early '90s that the pieces began to truly fit together for the Bulls. With the drafting of Scottie Pippen and Horace Grant, the Bulls assembled a core that would dominate the decade. The final piece of the puzzle was coach Phil Jackson, who implemented the triangle offense, a fluid and adaptable system that maximized the strengths of Jordan and Pippen and emphasized team play.

The Bulls' first championship in 1991 marked the beginning of a new era in the NBA. Jordan, Pippen, and the team showcased a blend of athleticism, skill, and intelligence that was previously unseen. The Bulls' first three championships from 1991 to 1993 were a tour de force, with Jordan's scoring prowess, defensive acumen, and clutch performances becoming legendary.

In a shocking twist that stunned the sports world, Michael Jordan retired from basketball in 1993 to play professional baseball. This left the Bulls without their leader and the NBA without its biggest star. While Jordan pursued a childhood dream in memory of his late father, the Bulls managed to remain competitive but were unable to capture another championship during his absence.

Jordan's return to the NBA in 1995 was heralded with two simple words: "I'm back." His return reignited the Bulls' championship aspirations. The 1995-1996 season saw the Bulls set a then-record of

72 wins, a testament to the team's dominance. The Bulls, with the addition of Dennis Rodman, another key component to their success, achieved their second three-peat from 1996 to 1998. This period was marked by Jordan's indomitable will to win, clutch performances in crucial moments, and a relentless pursuit of perfection.

The 1997-1998 Bulls, chronicled in the documentary "The Last Dance," faced a season filled with tension and speculation that it would be the last run for this group. Yet, despite the off-court distractions, the team remained focused, culminating in a sixth championship after a hard-fought battle against the Utah Jazz. Michael Jordan's game-winning shot in Game 6 of the finals is etched in basketball lore, a fitting finale to the Bulls' dynasty.

The Jordan-led Bulls not only amassed a staggering six championships in eight years but also helped globalize the game of basketball. Jordan became an icon transcending sport, and the team's influence was felt in the rise of international NBA players who grew up idolizing the Bulls. The team set the benchmark for excellence, and their influence extended beyond the hardwood, impacting the culture of sports, fashion, and media.

While championships are often the measure of success, the Jordan era Bulls' cultural impact was immeasurable. They inspired a generation of players and fans, changed how athletes are marketed, and contributed significantly to the NBA's global expansion. Jordan's legacy, coupled with the tenacity of Pippen, the zen mastery of coach Jackson, and the colorful character of Rodman, created an era of basketball that was as much about the spectacle and narrative as it was about the sport itself.

The Chicago Bulls' Jordan era represents more than a list of titles; it signifies a time where basketball became a global phenomenon, and a single team from the Windy City was its most captivating ambassador. It was an era where every game was a must-watch event, and every season ended with the expectation of a championship parade. The resonance of those championship years continues to echo throughout the corridors of the United Center and in the hearts of basketball fans around the world.

San Antonio Spurs: Consistency and Culture

The San Antonio Spurs, an exemplary model of consistency in the NBA, have woven an impressive tapestry of success since their entry into the league in 1976. Their story is one of strategic planning, a steadfast commitment to fundamental basketball, and a culture that has become the envy of the basketball world.

The Spurs' first stroke of championship destiny came with the drafting of David Robinson in 1987. The "Admiral" would become the cornerstone of the franchise, leading them to consistent playoff appearances. The arrival of Tim Duncan in 1997, known for his stoic demeanor and clinical play, formed the legendary "Twin Towers," setting the stage for their first NBA title in 1999.

The partnership of coach Gregg Popovich and Tim Duncan would evolve into one of the most successful coach-player duos in history. Under Popovich's leadership, the Spurs developed a playing style that valued ball movement, selflessness, and defensive rigor. With Duncan at the helm, they claimed championships in 2003, 2005, 2007, and 2014. Each title run was characterized by a relentless pursuit of perfection and a trust in the system Popovich designed.

What set the Spurs apart during their years of dominance was their global scouting acumen. They built an internationally diverse roster that included French maestro Tony Parker and Argentine dynamo Manu Ginóbili. Both players brought distinct playing styles that complemented Duncan's grounded presence and became key figures in the Spurs' championship narrative.

The Spurs' fifth championship in 2014 was a masterclass in team basketball, often cited as one of the purest examples of the sport. They faced the Miami Heat in a rematch of the previous year's finals, but this time, they played with a level of cohesion and selflessness that was unmatched, winning the series 4-1. This series was a testament to the Spurs' culture, showcasing their ability to elevate team play over individual stardom.

A hallmark of the Spurs' legacy has been their developmental system. They have been lauded for their ability to draft and develop talent, often turning late draft picks into key contributors. The Spurs' culture has also been defined by their loyalty and the long-term retention of their core players and coaching staff, which is increasingly rare in the modern era of the NBA.

Tim Duncan, often referred to as "The Big Fundamental," exemplified the Spurs' ethos throughout his 19-year career. His quiet leadership, combined with his relentless consistency on the court, earned him a reputation as one of the greatest power forwards of all time. Duncan's legacy is not only defined by his individual accolades but also by his ability to elevate the team above himself.

The San Antonio Spurs' approach to building a team and fostering a winning culture has had a profound impact on the league. They have shown that a small-market team can compete at the highest levels through smart management, player development, and a commitment to collective achievement. Their influence can be seen in how other teams approach both team construction and the cultivation of a winning culture.

In many ways, the Spurs' brand of basketball is a blueprint for success—a blueprint that prioritizes the whole over the individual, strategic foresight over impulsive decisions, and long-term success over fleeting triumphs. The San Antonio Spurs' consistency and culture have not just brought them championships; they have brought them a revered place in basketball history as a franchise that did it "the right way."

The Detroit Pistons: The Bad Boys

The story of the Detroit Pistons in the late 1980s is one of grit, tenacity, and an unyielding desire to disrupt the status quo of the NBA. Under the leadership of coach Chuck Daly, the Pistons transformed from a middling franchise into a formidable force, known to the world as the "Bad Boys" of basketball.

The Bad Boys Pistons were not just a team; they were a mentality. They played with a level of physicality and mental toughness that was unprecedented in the league at the time. The Pistons' philosophy was simple: make every opponent's trip to the basket a journey fraught with challenges, and never shy away from the physical aspect of the game. This intimidating style of play became their hallmark and was a stark contrast to the finesse teams of that era.

The Pistons' roster was carefully constructed to embody their physical philosophy. Isiah Thomas led the team with a unique combination of grace and grit. Joe Dumars provided steady scoring and tenacious defense. Bill Laimbeer and Rick Mahorn were the enforcers, patrolling the paint with an iron fist. Dennis Rodman brought an unmatched level of energy and defensive prowess, while Vinnie Johnson, the "Microwave," provided instant offense off the bench.

Detroit's path to championship glory was one of resilience. They climbed the ladder of success by toppling giants. In the late '80s, the Pistons had to overcome formidable foes, most notably the Boston Celtics and the Los Angeles Lakers, who had dominated the decade. The Pistons' back-to-back championships in 1989 and 1990 were a direct result of outlasting these powerhouses through sheer determination and a relentless defensive approach.

The 1989 championship run was particularly symbolic of the Pistons' evolution. They swept the Los Angeles Lakers, who were the defending champions and widely regarded as the team of the '80s. This sweep was not just a victory; it was a statement that the Pistons were the new power in the NBA.

The legacy of the Bad Boys Pistons is multi-faceted. They changed how defense was played in the NBA, emphasizing physicality and mental toughness. Their approach to the game influenced the defensive strategies of subsequent generations of coaches and players.

The Bad Boys also left a mark on the culture of basketball. They showed that a team could take on the identity of its city — hardworking, blue-collar, and unapologetic. Detroit embraced the Bad Boys, seeing in them the same resilience and determination that defined the city itself.

The Bad Boys era transcended sports, becoming a cultural phenomenon. They challenged the aesthetic of basketball at the time, which was characterized by high-flying dunks and fast-paced offense. They introduced a counter-narrative, one where defense, teamwork, and toughness were equally captivating and championship-worthy.

The reign of the Bad Boys would eventually come to an end, but not before leaving an indelible mark on the NBA. The lessons from their dominance would resonate throughout the league for years to come. Teams began to place a premium on defensive specialists and enforcers, roles that were epitomized by the Pistons of that era.

The Detroit Pistons' "Bad Boys" chapter is a crucial part of NBA history, illustrating that while skill and finesse are valuable, heart, toughness, and the will to win are just as vital to secure a place among the legends of the game.

International Clubs: Powerhouses of Passion

Basketball's international appeal is perhaps best exemplified by the vibrant and competitive leagues across Europe. Clubs like Real Madrid and FC Barcelona are not just football powerhouses but also dominate on the basketball court. Their participation in Spain's Liga ACB and the continental EuroLeague underscores the multifaceted nature of these sports giants.

Real Madrid Baloncesto: More Than Just Football

Real Madrid's basketball team, often overshadowed by its football counterpart, has a storied past that rivals any club in Europe. Founded in 1931, Real Madrid Baloncesto quickly became a mainstay in Spanish basketball, amassing a significant number of national league titles. The club's success is not limited to domestic competitions, as it boasts numerous EuroLeague championships, making it one of the most successful teams in the history of European basketball.

FC Barcelona Bàsquet: The Blaugrana on the Hardwood

FC Barcelona's basketball division has also cultivated a legacy of excellence. Established in 1926, they have a history steeped in success and are perennial contenders in both the Liga ACB and the EuroLeague. Their basketball section embodies the same spirit of competitiveness and excellence that the football team is known for, with a deep commitment to nurturing talent through its renowned La Masia academy, which extends beyond football to its other sports sections.

Greek Titans: Olympiacos and Panathinaikos

In Greece, a country with a fierce passion for basketball, two teams stand out: Olympiacos and Panathinaikos. These clubs share one of the most intense rivalries in sports, extending their contentious relationship to the basketball court. Their games, known as the "Derby of the Eternal Enemies," are highly anticipated events that often determine the fate of the Greek Basket League and have significant implications in EuroLeague standings.

Panathinaikos, with its numerous Greek League titles and EuroLeague victories, has a reputation for being a crucible of talent, producing some of Europe's most skilled players. On the other hand, Olympiacos has consistently demonstrated resilience and a knack for spectacular comebacks, securing its place in the pantheon of European basketball royalty.

CSKA Moscow: The Red Army's Sporting Pride

CSKA Moscow, often referred to as the "Red Army" team, has been a dominant force in Russian basketball since its inception. With a history that intertwines with the Soviet era, CSKA Moscow has been synonymous with excellence, frequently topping the Russian Premier League and making deep runs in the EuroLeague. The club's commitment to basketball excellence is evident in its state-of-the-art training facilities and the acquisition of top-tier international talent to complement its homegrown stars.

The EuroLeague: Europe's Premier Basketball Competition

The EuroLeague serves as the battleground where these titans clash. It is the pinnacle of European club basketball, a competition where history, passion, and the pursuit of glory come together. The league has seen legendary moments and has been a launching pad for players to make the leap to the NBA. It's a showcase of not just athletic prowess but also of strategic finesse, where coaches are as celebrated as the athletes themselves.

South American Fervor

Basketball club fervor is not confined to Europe. In South America, teams like Flamengo in Brazil and San Lorenzo in Argentina carry the torch for the sport. These clubs enjoy passionate fan bases and have developed a robust rivalry within their domestic leagues and the continental Liga Sudamericana.

These international clubs illustrate that the heart of basketball beats strongly around the world. They are more than just teams; they are institutions that represent the dreams and aspirations of their cities and countries. Each club, with its unique history and culture, contributes to the rich tapestry of international basketball, promoting a shared love for the game that transcends borders and languages.

Whether it's the storied histories of European powerhouses or the passionate support of South American clubs, international basketball is a testament to the sport's global reach and its power to unite people through their love of the game.

The Harlem Globetrotters: Ambassadors of Goodwill

The Harlem Globetrotters, with their inception in the 1920s, have evolved into a basketball institution synonymous with entertainment, athleticism, and ambassadorship. Despite their name, the team actually originated in Chicago and was formed by Abe Saperstein. They adopted the name "Harlem" to associate with the cultural hub that was renowned for its African American community and for being a center of jazz music and culture.

Their journey is not just one of entertainment but also of breaking racial barriers. During a time when the NBA was still segregated, the Globetrotters played a crucial role in introducing the talent of African American players to the world. They showed that skill and sportsmanship could transcend race, leading the way for the integration of professional basketball.

On the court, the Harlem Globetrotters are masters of the game, known for their exceptional ball-handling skills, basketball wizardry, and unrivaled flair. They have dazzled fans with their unique combination of sports and performance art, often engaging with the audience and incorporating comedic routines into their play. Yet, beneath the surface of their light-hearted performances lies a deeply competitive spirit and a profound love for basketball.

The Globetrotters have been more than a sports team; they've been cultural icons. They've appeared in films, on television shows, and even had their own animated series. Their red, white, and blue basketballs have bounced on the courts of over 120 countries, often in places where professional basketball was not yet established. They've met popes, kings, and countless dignitaries, serving as unconventional but effective diplomats.

Their legacy extends to their impact on the broader game of basketball. Many of their players, like Wilt Chamberlain, have gone on to have significant careers in the NBA. The Globetrotters have also been innovators, popularizing moves like the slam dunk and the behind-the-back pass, which are now staples in modern basketball playbooks.

The Harlem Globetrotters' most enduring quality is their ability to connect with fans from all walks of life. Their performances often transcend the game's outcome, focusing on joy, laughter, and the shared human experience. They've visited schools, hospitals, and orphanages, bringing smiles and hope to those who might need it most.

Today, the Harlem Globetrotters continue to evolve, embracing new generations of players and fans. They are committed to pushing the boundaries of what a basketball team can be, not just within the confines of a court but as global entertainers and goodwill ambassadors. The Harlem Globetrotters remain a vibrant reminder of basketball's power to entertain, inspire, and bring people together, regardless of background or borders.

The Harlem Globetrotters are much more than a basketball team; they are a symbol of the joyous spirit of the game, a touchstone in sports history, and a dynamic example of basketball's global language that speaks to the hearts of fans young and old alike.

Women's Basketball Clubs: Pioneers and Powerhouses

Women's basketball has seen its own set of influential clubs, particularly within the WNBA, which was founded in 1996. The Houston Comets not only became the league's first champions but went on to claim the title in the first four seasons (1997-2000), establishing the first dynasty in the WNBA. Led by stars like Cynthia Cooper, Sheryl Swoopes, and Tina Thompson, the Comets set the standard for excellence in the league and played a vital role in gaining attention and respect for women's professional basketball.

As the WNBA grew, so did the competition. Teams like the Minnesota Lynx emerged as a new force, with a model of consistency and team-oriented basketball. Led by players like Maya Moore, Seimone Augustus, and Lindsay Whalen, and under the guidance of coach Cheryl Reeve, the Lynx clinched multiple championships, cementing their place in the WNBA history books.

The Seattle Storm have also made their mark with superstars like Sue Bird and Lauren Jackson, known for their intelligent play and clutch performances. The Storm have consistently fielded competitive teams, capturing several championships and remaining a perennial threat in the playoffs.

While the WNBA has been the face of women's professional basketball in the United States, the international scene has been equally competitive. Clubs like UMMC Ekaterinburg and Dynamo Kursk in Russia have become hotspots for global talent, attracting stars from the WNBA and other leagues during the off-season. UMMC Ekaterinburg, in particular, has been a juggernaut in the EuroLeague Women's competition, boasting a roster filled with all-stars and Olympians, leading to multiple championships.

European women's basketball clubs have been instrumental in the development of the game globally. Teams like Fenerbahçe in Turkey and Perfumerías Avenida in Spain have been central to their national leagues and competitive in European play. These clubs not only compete for championships but also contribute to the growth of the sport by fostering young talent and providing a stage for players to showcase their skills on an international platform.

Moving beyond Europe, women's basketball in Asia and Oceania has seen significant growth. Clubs like the Southside Flyers in Australia's WNBL and the Shanghai Swordfish in China's WCBA have raised the profile of women's basketball in their regions. They've produced elite talent that competes in international competitions and often features in the WNBA.

The importance of women's basketball clubs extends beyond the court. They serve as pillars in the fight for gender equality in sports, pushing for better pay, more media coverage, and respect for women athletes. The success of these clubs not only inspires the next generation of female basketball players but also underlines the importance of providing equal opportunities for women in sports.

Looking to the future, women's basketball clubs continue to push the envelope, improving the quality of play, professionalism, and visibility of the women's game. They are not just participants in the sport; they are trendsetters and important cultural institutions that reflect the evolution of basketball as a whole.

Women's basketball clubs, whether in the WNBA or the international leagues, play a critical role in the development of the sport, the empowerment of women athletes, and the ongoing pursuit of equality and recognition in the world of professional sports.

The Power of Stories and Success in Basketball's Tapestry

Basketball's most endearing tales often come from the unexpected rise of the underdog—the teams that defy odds and overcome adversity. These narratives capture the hearts of fans and the essence of the sport. Clubs like the Golden State Warriors, before their rise to a modern dynasty, were once underdogs, with a history of struggles that made their ascent to championship glory all the more thrilling. Fans cherish the seasons where a team like the 2015 Warriors, led by the sharpshooting of Stephen Curry, upended the established hierarchy, creating a narrative that would define a generation.

Conversely, the dominance of dynasties such as the Chicago Bulls in the '90s and the Los Angeles Lakers and Boston Celtics throughout the decades constructs a different kind of story—one of sustained excellence and the setting of benchmarks. These teams do not just win titles; they craft eras that become the measuring sticks for greatness in the sport. The culture of these clubs, infused with the ethos of their star players and the strategic minds of their coaches, extends beyond the court and influences everything from sports apparel to the social and cultural conversations of the time.

The stories of basketball clubs also resonate through their impact on communities. Teams like the San Antonio Spurs have become synonymous with community engagement, creating strong bonds with their fans through inclusive and supportive initiatives. The narrative here is about legacy, but not just in terms of championships—rather, it is about the legacy of contributing to the social fabric of their home cities and creating a family beyond the roster.

The legends of basketball clubs are not confined to their immediate successes but live on through the inspiration they provide to future generations. The 'Showtime' Lakers of the '80s not only redefined the entertainment value of basketball but also inspired a young Kobe Bryant, who would one day don the purple and gold and forge his own era of excellence. Similarly, the stories of teams like the Detroit Pistons' "Bad Boys" have become cautionary yet iconic tales that resonate with both the players who remember their reign and the youth who learn about them through documentaries and retrospectives.

Basketball clubs evolve, and with each season, their stories take on new chapters. This constant evolution ensures that the narratives remain fresh and relevant. The New York Knicks' storied past, filled with moments of brilliance and periods of drought, speaks to the resilience not only of the team but also of their unwavering fan base. The identity of such a club is not static; it is shaped and reshaped by the players, the city, and the era, creating an ongoing story that is as much about the anticipation of future glory as it is about the nostalgia of past triumphs.

The stories of basketball clubs are also immortalized through memorabilia and media. Jerseys, sneakers, and posters become artifacts that carry the essence of a team's history. Films, books, and social media have allowed these stories to proliferate, ensuring that the narratives of teams like the Harlem Globetrotters, with their unique blend of sport and entertainment, reach audiences far and wide, preserving their legacy and influence for years to come.

The power of stories and success in basketball is immense, and the clubs at the heart of these stories are more than just teams—they are institutions that hold the collective memories, aspirations, and spirit of the sport. Their stories, woven into the larger narrative of basketball, continue to inspire and shape the game in ways that are profound and lasting.

The Evolution of Teams: Charting Basketball's Growth Through Club History

Basketball clubs have been integral to the social fabric of their times, often reflecting the triumphs and struggles of society. A prime example is the integration of the NBA, with pioneers like Earl Lloyd, Chuck Cooper, and Nat "Sweetwater" Clifton, who were among the first African Americans to play in the league. Their entrance into the NBA in the 1950s was not just about sport—it was a pivotal moment in the Civil Rights Movement, symbolizing broader societal changes and opening doors for future generations.

The story of team evolution is also the story of basketball's internationalization. In the 1980s and 1990s, players like Dražen

Petrović, Vlade Divac, and Hakeem Olajuwon brought global flavors to the NBA, influencing the style of play and opening the league to a new world of possibilities. Their success paved the way for the modern game, where international players like Luka Dončić and Giannis Antetokounmpo are among the league's biggest stars, and clubs routinely scout talent from every corner of the globe.

The evolution of women's basketball clubs has been another crucial chapter in the game's growth. With the founding of the WNBA in 1997 and the increasing visibility of women's collegiate basketball, clubs have become platforms for empowerment and excellence in women's sports. Teams like the Los Angeles Sparks and the Indiana Fever have carved out their own legacies, with players like Lisa Leslie, Tamika Catchings, and more recently, Breanna Stewart, becoming household names and inspiring young girls to take up the sport.

As basketball has advanced, so have the strategies employed by clubs. The introduction of video analysis and advanced metrics has revolutionized the way teams prepare for games and evaluate talent. Clubs have evolved from relying on intuition to utilizing data-driven approaches to gain competitive advantages, altering the tactical landscape of the sport.

The commercial evolution of basketball teams has been staggering. Clubs have become more than sports teams; they are now global brands. The Chicago Bulls' brand exploded internationally with the fame of Michael Jordan, and the Los Angeles Lakers and Boston Celtics have leveraged their storied histories to become synonymous with success. These teams market not only the game but also a lifestyle and culture that resonates worldwide.

The digital age has transformed how clubs engage with fans. Social media has allowed teams to create communities online, extending their reach and influence far beyond their geographic location. This has been crucial in driving the popularity of the game and has given fans unprecedented access to players and insider perspectives.

On a more local level, clubs have significantly impacted their home cities, contributing to urban development and community building. New stadiums and facilities become landmarks and centers of economic activity, revitalizing neighborhoods and creating a sense of pride and unity among residents.

In the face of global challenges, clubs are also evolving to become more sustainable and environmentally conscious. Initiatives to reduce carbon footprints and promote green practices are becoming more prevalent in the operations of basketball clubs. Additionally, the rise of e-sports and virtual reality is opening up new avenues for clubs to engage with fans and expand their brands into digital frontiers.

The evolution of basketball teams reflects the dynamic nature of the sport itself—constantly adapting, shifting, and growing. Clubs are more than players on a court; they are living entities that embody the history, culture, and future of basketball. As the game continues to expand, the stories of these teams will evolve, reflecting the changing face of basketball and its unifying spirit that resonates across the globe.

Chapter 7:
Biographies of Basketball Legends: Stories of the Greatest Players

The history of basketball is filled with the extraordinary exploits of players who didn't just master the game, they redefined it. Their remarkable talents have turned courts into stages for some of the most exhilarating dramas in sports. But the influence of these legendary figures extends beyond the hardwood boundaries of the basketball court, reaching into the very fabric of cultural and social realms. This chapter isn't just a recounting of achievements and statistical milestones—it's an exploration into the lives of individuals who became symbols of excellence, perseverance, and transformation.

In the quest to understand greatness, one must venture beyond the highlights and delve into the origins, the pivotal moments of adversity, and the crescendos of triumph. The stories of these basketball titans are laced with the sweat of unfathomable hours in gymnasiums, the emotional intensity of personal and team challenges, and the brilliance of moments when time seemed to stand still and the world bore witness to their genius.

As we turn the pages of their storied careers, we unravel how these players became much more than athletes. They became icons, leaders, and ambassadors, influencing fashion, language, attitudes, and values. They shaped identities, brought communities together, and at times, stood at the forefront of sociopolitical change. Through their journeys, we see the reflection of an evolving society, the breaking down of barriers, and the unifying power of sport.

Each player's narrative is a thread in the broader tapestry of basketball's legacy. Their footsteps have left indelible marks not only on the court but also in the hearts and minds of millions who dream of one day emulating their feats. Their stories are a testament to the human capacity to aspire and achieve, to fall and rise, to inspire and be inspired. As we recount the lives of these exceptional individuals, we pay homage to their contributions to the game and recognize their everlasting impact on the culture.

This chapter is a journey through time and across the globe, tracing the arcs of players who have become synonymous with basketball greatness. From the blacktops of inner cities to the glitz of professional arenas, from groundbreaking firsts to enduring legacies, we uncover the essence of what makes a basketball player not just a champion, but a legend. Welcome to the pantheon of the greatest players to ever grace the game of basketball, where each story is a unique chapter in the grand narrative of the sport.

Michael Jordan: The Flight of Air Jordan

The saga of Michael Jordan, often referred to as "MJ" or "Air Jordan," is one of basketball's most compelling narratives. Born on February 17, 1963, in Brooklyn, New York, Michael Jeffrey Jordan was the fourth of five children. His family moved to Wilmington, North Carolina, when he was a young child, a place that would become the proving grounds for his legendary work ethic. It was here, amidst the backdrop of Southern basketball culture, that Jordan began to forge his path.

Jordan attended Emsley A. Laney High School in Wilmington, where a significant event would fuel his competitive fire for years to come: being cut from the varsity basketball team during his sophomore year. This setback became a pivotal point in Jordan's life, one that he would later credit with instilling in him the resolve to exceed expectations. He dedicated himself to practice with a passion that became the hallmark of his career. The following summer, he grew several inches and trained rigorously, returning to earn a spot on the varsity team and immediately making an impact.

Jordan's college career at the University of North Carolina at Chapel Hill under the tutelage of Coach Dean Smith was marked by both individual growth and team success. In his freshman year, he made the game-winning shot in the 1982 NCAA Championship game against Georgetown, which featured another future NBA legend, Patrick Ewing. This moment was more than a clutch basket; it was a portent of the clutch performances that would come to define Jordan's career.

74

Entering the NBA in 1984 as the third overall draft pick by the Chicago Bulls, Jordan quickly established himself as a league standout. His rookie season performance earned him the NBA Rookie of the Year Award, and he was selected for the All-Star Game—an honor he would receive 14 times in his career.

Michael Jordan's influence on the game was seismic. His scoring prowess, showcased by a record ten scoring titles, was matched only by his defensive intensity, evidenced by nine All-Defensive First Team honors. His leaping ability and acrobatic maneuvers in the air earned him the nickname "Air Jordan" and inspired the iconic "Jumpman" logo.

Jordan's determination to win was never more apparent than in the postseason. He led the Bulls to two three-peats of NBA Championships in the 1990s, from 1991 to 1993 and again from 1996 to 1998, a feat that has become a benchmark for modern basketball dynasties. He was named NBA Finals MVP in each of these championships, a testament to his ability to perform at the highest level when the stakes were greatest.

Jordan's reach extended beyond the court. His endorsements, including a longstanding relationship with Nike, led to a line of sneakers and apparel that transformed the marketing of athlete brands. His starring role in the movie "Space Jam" brought together entertainment and sports in an unprecedented way, further cementing his status as a pop culture icon.

Off the court, Jordan has been a businessman and owner, purchasing a controlling interest in the Charlotte Hornets and influencing the business side of the NBA. His charitable contributions and dedication to social issues have also contributed to his legacy.

Michael Jordan's biography isn't merely a chronicle of games won or points scored—it's a narrative of a man who reshaped the contours of his sport and inspired a generation to "Be Like Mike." His competitive spirit, commitment to excellence, and transcendent talent have left an indelible mark on the world of sports. Even after his retirement, his influence lingers in the aspirations of young players across the globe and in the continued popularity of his brand. Jordan remains, for many, the embodiment of basketball greatness, a symbol of the heights that human potential can reach when paired with an unyielding desire to succeed.

Bill Russell: The Ultimate Winner

Bill Russell's story begins in Monroe, Louisiana, on February 12, 1934. Growing up in the segregated South before his family moved to the more racially tolerant Oakland, California, Russell faced challenges that would forge his resilience and strength of character. His experiences with racism and poverty shaped not only his views on society but also his determination to excel in all facets of life.

During his years at McClymonds High School in Oakland, Russell's athletic talent became apparent, although not immediately in basketball. He found his first successes in track and field as a high jumper. His leap into basketball prominence began in earnest when he learned to channel his exceptional defensive instincts and leaping ability into the sport.

Russell attended the University of San Francisco (USF), where he would lead the Dons to two consecutive NCAA championships in 1955 and 1956. Russell's defensive skills were revolutionary. His ability to block shots and dominate rebounds turned defensive play into an offensive weapon, altering the course of basketball strategy forever.

Drafted by the Boston Celtics in 1956, Russell became the cornerstone of the most storied dynasty in NBA history under the guidance of coach Red Auerbach. Russell's rivalry with Wilt Chamberlain, another all-time great, provided some of the most compelling competitions in sports history. However, it was Russell's unselfish play and focus on team success that yielded an unprecedented 11 NBA championships during his 13-year career, including eight in a row from 1959 to 1966.

Off the court, Russell was a titan of social justice. He participated in the 1963 March on Washington and stood with Muhammad Ali during the Cleveland Summit in 1967. Russell's refusal to tolerate racism manifested in several incidents where he confronted inequality, such as when he led a Celtics boycott of a game in Lexington, Kentucky, after a restaurant refused to serve the team's Black players.

Bill Russell also broke barriers in coaching, becoming the first African American head coach in any major U.S. sport and the first to win a championship. His impact on the game of basketball is measured not only in his copious championships and five MVP awards but also in the way he demonstrated that an athlete could be a catalyst for change.

Russell's mentoring of younger players and his intellectual approach to the game have left lasting marks on countless individuals. His commitment to team success over individual glory has become a benchmark for what it means to be a great teammate.

Russell's death in 2022 was not just the passing of an NBA legend but the loss of a monumental figure in American history. His autobiography, "Go Up for Glory," and other writings offer deep insight into his philosophy on life and competition. His legacy as a winner is unparalleled in professional team sports, but his truest victory lies in the strides he made for civil rights and the path he forged for athletes to use their voices for meaningful change. Bill Russell remains a beacon for what it means to be a champion, both in sports and in the pursuit of a more just society.

Kareem Abdul-Jabbar: More Than Just the Skyhook

Kareem Abdul-Jabbar, born Ferdinand Lewis Alcindor Jr. on April 16, 1947, in New York City, grew up in the towering shadows of the Harlem Renaissance. This cultural milieu, along with his towering physical height, shaped his perspective and ambitions. From a young age, Lew, as he was known then, exhibited not only extraordinary athletic talent but also a deep intellectual curiosity.

Abdul-Jabbar's basketball journey gained national attention at UCLA, where he played under legendary coach John Wooden. His impact was immediate and transformative; the Bruins dominated college basketball, winning three consecutive national championships from 1967 to 1969. Alcindor's combination of size, skill, and basketball IQ made him an unstoppable force, prompting the NCAA to ban the dunk for nine years, partly in response to his dominance.

Entering the NBA in 1969, he quickly became a force for the Milwaukee Bucks, bringing them an NBA championship in his second season. His transition from Lew Alcindor to Kareem Abdul-Jabbar marked not just a personal transformation in embracing Islam but also a cultural shift that reflected the changing landscape of America.

Abdul-Jabbar's skyhook was a poetic embodiment of his play — an amalgamation of grace, precision, and effectiveness. However, his contributions to the game go beyond his scoring prowess. He was an excellent defender, passer, and team leader, characteristics that anchored the Los Angeles Lakers during their Showtime era in the 1980s.

Off the court, Abdul-Jabbar has been a renaissance man. His voice has resonated in the op-ed sections of newspapers, in the halls of museums as a curator, and in the lines of the many books he has authored. His writing and activism have touched upon issues of race, religion, and social justice, providing thoughtful insights grounded in a deep understanding of history.

Kareem's commitment to education and youth mentorship further illustrates his multifaceted impact. He has been involved in numerous projects, including the Skyhook Foundation, which aims to inspire children in underserved communities by providing educational opportunities in STEM fields.

His NBA records, which include the second most points scored in league history, six MVP awards, and six championships, are a testament to his long-term excellence and adaptability. His All-Star appearances spanned three different decades, showcasing his ability to remain at the pinnacle of the sport through massive changes in the pace and style of play.

Now, as a recipient of the Presidential Medal of Freedom, Abdul-Jabbar stands as a figure whose impact transcends basketball. His social commentary and advocacy continue to challenge and inspire. From speaking out against discrimination to advocating for cancer research after his own battle with the disease, Abdul-Jabbar's legacy is as layered and profound as his fabled skyhook — an inspiration that continues to resonate in arenas far beyond the hardwood of the basketball court.

Magic Johnson: The Magic Man's Showtime

Born Earvin Johnson Jr. on August 14, 1959, in Lansing, Michigan, the man who would become "Magic" was anointed with his nickname after a mesmerizing triple-double performance in high school. His captivating smile and effervescent personality were evident early on, and they became his trademarks alongside his exceptional basketball talent.

Magic's leap to fame was solidified at Michigan State University, where he led the Spartans to an NCAA Championship in 1979, setting the stage for a storied rivalry with Larry Bird that would span their professional careers. His entry into the NBA was no less dramatic, as he joined a Los Angeles Lakers team that was poised for greatness.

Johnson was a revolutionary force in the NBA, redefining what a point guard could be. Standing at an imposing 6'9", his physical stature was matched by an equally expansive vision of the court. He led the Lakers with a flair that married efficiency with entertainment, orchestrating the fast-paced "Showtime" offense that enthralled fans and overwhelmed opponents.

During his illustrious career, Magic captured five NBA championships and three MVP awards. His duels with Larry Bird and the Boston Celtics became the stuff of legend, a bicoastal rivalry that spurred the league to new heights of popularity and competition.

Magic's announcement in 1991 that he had contracted HIV was a seminal moment in sports and cultural history. At a time when the disease was mired in stigma and misunderstanding, Johnson's disclosure humanized the struggle against HIV/AIDS and brought unprecedented attention to the epidemic.

Following his retirement, Johnson transformed his challenges into advocacy, becoming a powerful force in the fight against HIV/AIDS. His Magic Johnson Foundation has been instrumental in educating the public, promoting testing, and supporting communities affected by the virus.

Beyond his health advocacy, Johnson's entrepreneurial spirit has flourished. He has become a successful businessman, investing in urban communities, bringing economic development, and providing jobs. His ventures range from movie theaters to Starbucks franchises, always with a focus on underrepresented areas.

Magic Johnson's legacy is a tapestry of high-octane basketball brilliance and profound societal impact. His Magic has extended beyond the hardwood, where his assists are no longer just about scoring but also about uplifting communities and fostering positive change. In boardrooms, charity events, and public initiatives, Johnson continues to embody the charisma and leadership that made him an icon of the sport.

Even in retirement, Johnson serves as a mentor to young athletes and a voice of wisdom in the sports community. His insights on leadership, resilience, and transformation are sought after by many, reflecting a life lived at the intersection of athletic excellence and dedicated philanthropy. Magic Johnson's story teaches that one can indeed inspire and lead in multiple arenas, and that true magic lies in the ability to elevate those around you.

Larry Bird: The Hick from French Lick

Larry Bird's saga begins in the small town of French Lick, Indiana, where he honed his skills in a high school gym that would become the crucible for his legendary work ethic and precision shooting. Born on December 7, 1956, Bird grew up in a blue-collar family, and his early life was marked by hardship and the gritty determination that would become his trademark.

Bird first drew national attention at Indiana State University, leading the Sycamores to the NCAA championship game in 1979 against none other than Magic Johnson's Michigan State, setting the stage for one of the greatest rivalries in sports history. Bird's college career laid the groundwork for his unshakable confidence and his relentless pursuit of victory.

Drafted into the NBA by the Boston Celtics in 1978, Bird immediately became the cornerstone of the franchise's renewal. Over the course of his 13-year career, he led the Celtics to three NBA championships and earned three consecutive MVP awards from 1984 to 1986—a feat only matched by a handful of players in the history of the league.

Bird's rivalry with Magic Johnson transcended the hardwood, capturing the imagination of fans and igniting a resurgence in the NBA's popularity. The contrast between Bird's stoic, blue-collar image and Magic's charismatic showmanship provided a compelling narrative that continued through multiple epic championship confrontations.

Larry Bird was not the most athletic player on the court, but he was often the smartest. Renowned for his basketball IQ, he had an uncanny ability to anticipate plays before they happened, seeing angles and opportunities that remained invisible to others until he unveiled them with a pinpoint pass or a timely shot.

Bird's reputation for clutch performances is legendary. Whether it was his confidence in taking the last-second shot or his remarkable come-from-behind victories, Bird seemed to thrive under pressure, cementing his status as one of the game's greatest closers.

After retiring as a player, Bird's impact on the game continued. He served as a successful coach and executive, bringing his understanding of the game and his unyielding standards to these roles. Under his leadership, both the Indiana Pacers and the Celtics experienced periods of success, demonstrating his versatility and basketball acumen.

Larry Bird's legacy is not just in the banners hanging from the rafters in Boston or the accolades in his trophy case. It is also in the countless players who have emulated his work ethic, his basketball intelligence, and his competitive fire. Bird's journey from the small town of French Lick to the pinnacle of basketball success is a testament to the power of dedication, skill, and the unrelenting desire to win.

Bird's connection to his Indiana roots remained strong throughout his career and into his post-playing days. His life and career stand as a testament to the values of the heartland: hard work, perseverance, and an uncompromising commitment to excellence. Larry Bird, The Hick from French Lick, is a quintessential American sports story, embodying the spirit of determination that resonates with basketball fans and beyond.

Wilt Chamberlain: The Record-Breaking Giant

Born on August 21, 1936, in Philadelphia, Pennsylvania, Wilton Norman Chamberlain was a towering figure both in stature and in talent from a young age. At Overbrook High School, Chamberlain's prodigious skills were evident as he amassed points and rebounds at a rate the city had never seen before. His high school performances were a prelude to a career that would be marked by statistical astonishments and superhuman anecdotes.

Chamberlain's collegiate career at the University of Kansas heralded the arrival of a player who could dominate the game in a manner previously unseen. Although his team fell short in the NCAA championship, his presence was so impactful that it led to changes in college basketball rules, including widening the lane to neutralize players with Chamberlain's size and skill—a testament to his game-changing ability.

In the NBA, Chamberlain's physical gifts translated into unparalleled success. His most iconic moment came on March 2, 1962, when he scored an unprecedented 100 points for the Philadelphia Warriors in a game against the New York Knicks. Chamberlain's battles against contemporaries like Bill Russell became the stuff of legend, providing a backdrop for the NBA's rise in popularity during the 1960s.

Chamberlain's name is scattered throughout the NBA record books. He holds numerous records, including the most points in a season, the highest average points per game in a season, and the most rebounds in a game. His astonishing feat of averaging more than 50 points a game during the 1961-1962 season remains a benchmark of individual excellence.

Despite his scoring prowess, Chamberlain's contributions extended beyond mere points. He led the league in rebounds 11 times and even led in assists once, a rare accomplishment for a center, as he sought to prove his versatility and unselfishness. He was a trailblazer in proving that a big man could be multi-dimensional on the court.

Chamberlain's quest for an NBA championship was fulfilled twice, first with the Philadelphia 76ers in 1967 and then with the Los Angeles Lakers in 1972. His presence on the court forced teams to innovate new strategies and defensive schemes, altering the course of basketball tactics forever.

Off the court, Chamberlain was as dynamic as he was on it. His engaging personality, coupled with his success in various ventures, including business and acting, made him a prominent figure in the cultural landscape of the 20th century. His autobiography "Wilt: Just Like Any Other 7-Foot Black Millionaire Who Lives Next Door" and his candidness about his personal life contributed to his lasting impact on popular culture.

Wilt Chamberlain passed away on October 12, 1999, but the stories of his incredible physical feats and competitive nature continue to be shared among basketball fans and athletes. He was a man who not only reshaped basketball but also left behind a legacy of what it means to push the boundaries of possibility. Chamberlain's legend is not merely preserved in the history of sports but in the collective memory of a giant who lived up to his mythic status in every way imaginable.

Kobe Bryant: The Mamba Mentality

Kobe Bean Bryant was born on August 23, 1978, in Philadelphia, Pennsylvania. The son of former NBA player Joe Bryant, Kobe's affinity for basketball was evident from an early age. After spending some of his formative years in Italy, where his father continued his professional career, Kobe's international experience enriched his approach to the game. Returning to the United States in high school, his prowess at Lower Merion High School in Pennsylvania garnered national attention, culminating in his decision to bypass college and declare for the NBA draft—a move that was rare at the time but paved the way for future generations.

Selected 13th overall by the Charlotte Hornets in the 1996 NBA Draft and promptly traded to the Los Angeles Lakers, Kobe would spend his entire 20-year career with the storied franchise. His journey with the Lakers was a saga filled with triumphs, challenges, and the relentless pursuit of greatness.

Kobe quickly became a marquee player, known for his scoring ability, acrobatic plays, and tenacious work ethic. The "Black Mamba," a nickname he gave himself after the agile and deadly African snake, encapsulated his approach to the game—striking with precision and performing at his best under pressure. His drive and determination were instrumental in the Lakers' three consecutive championships from 2000 to 2002, alongside Shaquille O'Neal, under the guidance of coach Phil Jackson.

After the dynasty's initial run, Kobe's career was marked by a quest to prove his capability as a leader and a primary option on championship teams. He achieved personal milestones, including an 81-point game in 2006, the second-highest single-game scoring performance in NBA history. His dedication delivered two more NBA titles in 2009 and 2010, with the latter championship notably including a Finals victory over the Boston Celtics, a fitting triumph in the historic Lakers-Celtics rivalry.

Kobe's impact extended beyond the hardwood. His interests in storytelling and content creation led to the founding of Granity Studios, a media company. His artistic endeavors were highlighted by his Academy Award for the animated short film "Dear Basketball," which brought to life his farewell poem to the sport he loved.

Beyond his scoring records and five championships, Kobe's legacy is deeply tied to his "Mamba Mentality"—a philosophy centered on the relentless pursuit of improvement. His tragic death on January 26, 2020, in a helicopter crash that also claimed the life of his daughter Gianna and seven others, sent shockwaves through the sports world and beyond.

Kobe's death prompted a global outpouring of grief and remembrance, underscoring his influence not only as an athlete but as a cultural icon. His approach to basketball and life continues to inspire athletes across all sports, as well as individuals striving to excel in their own endeavors.

Kobe Bryant's story is one of talent, ambition, and the uncompromising pursuit of one's passions. He remains a figure of inspiration, a testament to the power of dedication, and a reminder of the impact one individual can have on the game of basketball and the world. His legacy is not merely in the records or trophies but in the mindset he championed and the countless individuals he inspired to be their best selves.

LeBron James: The King's Court

LeBron Raymone James's journey to basketball royalty began on December 30, 1984, in Akron, Ohio. Raised by his single mother, Gloria James, LeBron faced numerous challenges that made his meteoric rise to stardom all the more remarkable. At St. Vincent-St. Mary High School, he was the focal point of national media attention, touted as the future of basketball—a prophecy he has more than fulfilled.

Drafted first overall in the 2003 NBA Draft by the Cleveland Cavaliers, LeBron quickly lived up to the hype, earning the Rookie of the Year award. His combination of size, speed, and vision revolutionized the forward position. He has been compared to legends like Michael Jordan and Magic Johnson, but LeBron's unique blend of talents has carved out a niche that's entirely his own.

LeBron's list of achievements is extensive: four MVP awards, multiple All-NBA First Team nods, two Olympic gold medals, and his ongoing presence as an All-Star. More significantly, he has led his teams to four NBA championships, with titles won with the Miami

Heat, Cleveland Cavaliers, and Los Angeles Lakers. Each championship run has its own narrative, from his "Decision" to take his talents to South Beach to his heartfelt promise to bring a title to his native Ohio, which he delivered in historic fashion in 2016.

Off the court, LeBron has taken the mantle of a social leader, unafraid to speak on critical issues affecting the African American community and beyond. His "I PROMISE School," an initiative in Akron for at-risk children, showcases his commitment to education and philanthropy. Furthermore, his More Than a Vote campaign reflects his engagement in the fight against voter suppression.

LeBron's interests extend into the business and entertainment sectors, where his savvy investments and production company, SpringHill Entertainment, have produced content that reflects his interests and values. His involvement in various ventures has positioned him as a role model for athlete-driven business success.

Even as he advances into the latter stages of his career, LeBron's influence on the court remains profound. His pursuit of excellence and adaptability has seen him refine his game, focusing on precision and intelligence as physical attributes evolve with age. The discussion of his place among the pantheon of greats continues with each passing season, as he cements his status as one of the most impactful players in basketball history.

LeBron's most enduring legacy may be his impact on future generations—how he has inspired young athletes to leverage their platforms for change and to never be confined to just one arena.

Whether it's through basketball, business, social activism, or cultural influence, LeBron James has redefined what it means to be an athlete in the 21st century.

In many ways, LeBron's story is still being written. As he continues to perform at an elite level, breaking records, and defying age, he remains at the forefront of basketball's evolving narrative. His drive to be the best in everything he does has made the name LeBron James synonymous with greatness, not just in basketball, but as an enduring symbol of excellence and influence in the broader spectrum of life.

Diana Taurasi: The White Mamba

Diana Lorena Taurasi, born on June 11, 1982, in Glendale, California, to Argentinian and Italian parents, was introduced to basketball at an early age. Her international roots would later play a significant role in her global appeal and understanding of the game. Taurasi's prowess became evident during her time at Don Lugo High School and continued as she dominated the college courts at the University of Connecticut. Under the tutelage of the legendary coach Geno Auriemma, Taurasi led UConn to three consecutive NCAA championships, showcasing her leadership and ability to perform under pressure.

Selected first overall in the 2004 WNBA draft by the Phoenix Mercury, Taurasi embarked on a professional career that would redefine excellence in women's basketball. She has since garnered an impressive list of accolades, including multiple WNBA MVP awards and All-Star selections, further punctuated by a collection of scoring titles that testify to her offensive prowess.

Her winning mentality translated to success with the USA Basketball Women's National Team as well. Taurasi has been instrumental in securing Olympic gold medals, affirming her status as one of the greatest to ever play the game.

Taurasi's international career is as decorated as her domestic one, with significant contributions to several prominent European teams. She has been a part of championship-winning squads in the EuroLeague, amassing individual honors and helping her teams achieve continental glory. This global experience has not only enhanced her skill set but has also allowed her to spread her influence to an international audience, serving as an ambassador for the women's game worldwide.

Nicknamed "The White Mamba" by Kobe Bryant, Taurasi's competitive fire is legendary. She's known for her intense desire to win and her unwillingness to back down in big moments. This tenacity has led her to hit some of the most memorable shots in WNBA history and has made her a beacon for clutch performance.

As a veteran leader, Taurasi has taken on the role of mentor to younger players in the league. Her guidance has been pivotal in developing the next generation of stars. Off the court, she's a vocal advocate for gender equality in sports, pushing for better pay and more media coverage for women's basketball.

Taurasi's career longevity is a testament to her dedication to maintaining her body and evolving her game. Her impact on the court remains undeniable, often leading her team in scoring and assists and her ability to play at a high level for so many years has set a standard for what is possible for female athletes in basketball and beyond.

Even as she writes new chapters in her storied career, Diana Taurasi's legacy is secure. Her name is synonymous with greatness in women's basketball, and her influence extends far beyond her on-court achievements. As a role model, a competitor, and a leader, Taurasi has paved the way for future generations, ensuring that her story will be told for decades to come as a shining example of excellence and the power of sports to change lives.

Lisa Leslie: Pioneering Height in Women's Basketball

Lisa Deshaun Leslie was born on July 7, 1972, in Gardena, California. Her athletic journey began on the playgrounds of Los Angeles and by the time she reached middle school, Leslie had already grown to over six feet tall, a stature that hinted at her basketball destiny. At Morningside High School in Inglewood, California, she blossomed into a star, famously scoring 101 points in a single half of a game. Her high school accomplishments set the stage for a storied career that would see her break barriers and set records at every level.

Leslie's prowess on the basketball court continued at the University of Southern California (USC), where she became an All-American and left a legacy of dominance. Her USC career is marked by numerous records and accolades, establishing her as one of the premier players in collegiate basketball and a force to be reckoned with in the paint.

When the WNBA was founded in 1996, Lisa Leslie was one of the original players and became the face of the league. Drafted by the Los Angeles Sparks, she would lead the team to two WNBA championships and earn three MVP awards throughout her career. Leslie's presence in the WNBA brought legitimacy and star power to the newly formed league, helping to cement its place in the professional sports landscape.

Leslie's impact wasn't confined to domestic play. She was a cornerstone of the USA Women's National Basketball Team, capturing four Olympic gold medals and becoming one of the most decorated athletes in Olympic basketball history. Her international success elevated the status of American women's basketball and inspired countless young athletes around the globe.

Leslie's versatility on the court was remarkable. She was the first player to dunk in a WNBA game, showcasing her athleticism and expanding the realm of possibility for female basketball players. Off the court, her leadership extended into her roles as a mentor, coach, and advocate for women's sports.

Leslie's contributions to basketball transcend her on-court achievements. She was the first woman to be honored with a statue outside the Staples Center in Los Angeles, a testament to her impact on the game and her role in advancing women's athletics. Her advocacy for women in sports has been a consistent theme throughout her career, pushing for equity and recognition.

After retiring from professional play, Leslie has remained a prominent figure in basketball and sports media. Her work as a commentator and analyst has provided insightful and authoritative perspectives on the game she helped shape. Leslie's autobiography, "Don't Let the Lipstick Fool You," and her foray into modeling and acting have shown the multidimensional aspects of her post-basketball life.

Lisa Leslie's legacy is one of groundbreaking achievements and lasting influence. She changed the perception of women's basketball, not only by her play but by her poise, professionalism, and unwavering commitment to excellence. As a player, coach, and ambassador of the game, Leslie has paved the way for the future of women's basketball, ensuring her story will continue to inspire for generations to come.

The stories of these basketball legends are not just about points scored or games won. They are about the human spirit's capacity to inspire, to overcome adversity, and to lead. Their biographies serve as blueprints for greatness and as reminders that the sport's true essence lies in its ability to elevate those who play it and those who love it. As the game of basketball evolves, the legends' narratives will continue to influence aspiring players and the broader sports culture for years to come.

Chapter 8:
The Most Amazing Games in Basketball History

asketball, at its core, is a symphony of moments—each second a potential seed of the miraculous. It's a game where buzzer-beaters shatter the hopes of one team and immortalize another in victory, where historic comebacks craft narratives of resilience, where record-breaking performances become benchmarks of excellence, and where contests are not merely played but etched deeply into the collective memory of fans and players alike. This chapter is an ode to those games that have transcended the typical bounds of sport, occasions where the tick of the clock paused, hearts collectively skipped beats, and players on the hardwood ascended into the realm of legends.

The Game of Change: 1966 NCAA Championship

On a spring evening in 1966, the NCAA Championship game was poised to transcend the boundaries of sport. Texas Western College (now the University of Texas at El Paso), led by coach Don Haskins, entered the final against Adolph Rupp's University of Kentucky Wildcats—a program that, until then, was an all-white powerhouse in college basketball.

The game was as much a cultural clash as it was a sporting event. Rupp's Wildcats represented the traditional basketball establishment, while Haskins' Miners were set to challenge the status quo. The Miners' all-African American starting lineup was a bold statement in an era of pervasive segregation, especially in the South.

As the game unfolded at the University of Maryland's Cole Field House, it became evident that Texas Western was not just playing for a title but also for the validation of talent regardless of color. The Miners' style, characterized by tenacious defense and team-oriented offense, began to dismantle the Wildcats' game plan. Every basket, every defensive stop by Texas Western was a rebuke to the barriers of segregation that had long plagued the country.

Texas Western's victory was decisive, a triumph that reverberated far beyond the collegiate basketball landscape. It was a victory for civil rights, a tangible demonstration that excellence knows no color. The Miners' win was a catalyst for change across athletic programs nationwide, accelerating the integration of sports at colleges and universities across the country.

The 1966 NCAA Championship game forced a reevaluation of prejudices and opened doors for black athletes not just in basketball but in all college sports. It challenged the perceptions of African American athletes' roles and capabilities, setting a new benchmark for what teams could aspire to be.

The significance of Texas Western's win cannot be overstated. It stands as a landmark moment in the civil rights movement, a point where the battle for equality found a new arena on the basketball court. The game has been immortalized in books, documentaries, and the film "Glory Road," ensuring that the story of the Miners' historic season and their contribution to the civil rights movement continues to inspire.

The 1966 NCAA Championship game is remembered not merely for the quality of basketball played but for its role in shaping the social fabric of America. It was a contest that highlighted the power of sports as a catalyst for social change and the enduring idea that courage on the court can lead to transformation off of it. The Miners' victory is etched in history as a triumph that extended well beyond the final buzzer, echoing through the generations as the Game of Change.

The Miracle at Madison Square Garden: Willis Reed's Heroic Comeback

The 1970 NBA Finals had already provided its share of drama and excitement, but nothing could have prepared fans for what they would witness in Game 7. The series between the New York Knicks and the Los Angeles Lakers had been a seesaw battle of basketball giants, but the Knicks' hopes seemed to be dashed when Willis Reed, their star center and emotional leader, suffered a severe thigh injury in Game 5 and missed Game 6.

As the decisive game approached, the question on every Knicks fan's mind was whether Willis Reed would play. Without him, the formidable task of containing Wilt Chamberlain seemed insurmountable. The atmosphere in Madison Square Garden was electric with anticipation, the crowd buzzing with a mixture of hope and anxiety.

Minutes before the game, the Knicks' locker room was shrouded in uncertainty until Reed, limping and in obvious pain, emerged from the tunnel. The Garden erupted in a roar of support. Reed's entrance is etched in the memory of every fan who witnessed it— a moment of pure fortitude and determination.

Reed started the game against all odds, and while his physical contribution was limited to those first two baskets, his presence on the floor had a galvanizing effect on his teammates. The Knicks were lifted by Reed's courage, playing with renewed vigor and intensity that transcended the game's typical strategy and skill.

While Reed's heroism is the enduring image, it was Walt Frazier who delivered an all-time great performance in the same game. His 36 points and 19 assists were instrumental in the Knicks' victory, though it was Reed's resilience that remained the emotional core of the win.

This Game 7 did more than decide a championship; it became a symbol of perseverance and heart. Willis Reed's heroics on that day in May 1970 have inspired countless players and teams to push beyond their perceived limits. It is a reminder that sometimes, the most significant victories in sports are not just achieved through talent but through an indomitable will.

The Miracle at Madison Square Garden is a tale passed down through generations, growing in legend with each retelling. It has become a benchmark for what it means to be a leader and a teammate. Reed's triumph over adversity is a story that resonates far beyond basketball, a testament to the human spirit's capacity to overcome and inspire.

The 1970 NBA Finals Game 7 is immortalized as one of the greatest moments in sports history, not just for the New York Knicks or the NBA, but for all of athletics. It is remembered as a night when an arena, a city, and the game of basketball itself were uplifted by one man's improbable return, a man who, in just a few minutes, captured the essence of competition and the power of sports to uplift and unite.

The 1976 NBA Finals: Triple-Overtime Thriller

The stage for this iconic game was the venerable Boston Garden, known for its intimate atmosphere and sweltering conditions, which only heightened the intensity of the Finals. With the series tied at two games apiece, Game 5 was more than just a pivotal matchup; it was the confluence of passion, skill, and sheer willpower, encapsulating the very essence of playoff basketball.

From the opening tip-off, the game was a seesaw battle of lead changes and ties. The Celtics, led by the indomitable Jo Jo White and the fiery Dave Cowens, traded blows with a resilient Suns team anchored by the sharpshooting of Paul Westphal and the tenacity of

Gar Heard. The game's intensity was palpable, with each possession carrying the weight of a potential championship.

The game's first 48 minutes were merely a prelude to the unprecedented drama that unfolded in the overtimes. A sequence of controversial calls, including a technical foul for calling a timeout when none were available, added to the chaos. The Suns' ability to tie the game with a buzzer-beater at the end of the second overtime by Gar Heard is etched in Finals lore, a shot known simply as "The Shot Heard 'Round the World."

As the game extended into its third overtime, it became a test of endurance, with players on both sides pushing their physical limits. The Garden's stifling air, the fatigue of the players, and the emotional rollercoaster of the game contributed to an atmosphere that was as surreal as it was electric.

Jo Jo White's performance in the triple-overtime periods, scoring 33 points over the course of the game, was emblematic of the Celtics' resilience. His poise under pressure and endurance over the course of a grueling 58 minutes of play were instrumental in securing the win for Boston.

When the final buzzer sounded, the Celtics emerged victorious in a 128-126 win, but the game's legacy was just beginning. It became an instant classic, often cited when discussing the greatest games in NBA history. The game served as a benchmark for what it means to compete at the highest level, and it remains a touchstone for the drama and beauty of professional basketball.

The 1976 NBA Finals Game 5 has been revisited countless times in highlight reels, documentaries, and discussions, each replay bringing to life the unparalleled excitement of that night. It stands as a testament to the players and the game itself, a reminder of why basketball captivates and thrills, and why some moments in sports are truly timeless.

More than just a game, the triple-overtime thriller between the Celtics and the Suns is a microcosm of basketball at its best— unpredictable, exhilarating, and filled with moments that remain imprinted in the memory of fans. This game, with its highs and lows, its heroes and villains, encapsulates the essence of the NBA and the unrelenting pursuit of greatness that defines the Finals. It remains a beacon of the sport, a standard-bearer for the heights basketball can reach and the depths of passion it can evoke.

Magic's Baby Skyhook: 1987 NBA Finals

The 1987 NBA Finals represented another chapter in the storied Lakers-Celtics rivalry that had defined the league's narrative for much of the 1980s. These two storied franchises once again found themselves vying for basketball supremacy. With the series shifting back and forth, Game 4 in the storied Boston Garden was more than just a game; it was potentially the turning point of the series.

As the game unfolded, it was a classic test of wills, pitting the Lakers' fast-paced "Showtime" style against the Celtics' gritty, determined play. The Lakers, having taken a series lead, were looking to place a stranglehold on the championship chase, while the Celtics were desperate to even the score and reclaim their home-court advantage.

The game was a tightly contested affair, with neither team able to gain a decisive advantage. As the clock wound down, the score was tied, and the Lakers had possession. Magic Johnson, already known for his big-game heroics and unparalleled versatility, took the inbounds pass and began to orchestrate the final play.

With just seconds remaining, Magic maneuvered into the paint, amidst a forest of Celtics' defenders, and lofted a delicate hook shot, a move he had borrowed from teammate Kareem Abdul-Jabbar, but with his unique touch. The ball arced gracefully over the outstretched hands of Boston's defenders and fell through the net. The "junior, junior skyhook," as it would come to be known, was a shot of audacious creativity and pinpoint execution.

The Celtics, stunned by the sudden turn of events, were unable to answer back, and the Lakers sealed a crucial victory, taking a 3-1 series lead. This moment was more than just a game-winner; it shifted the entire momentum of the Finals, effectively quelling the Celtics' resurgence and paving the way for the Lakers' eventual championship victory.

Magic's skyhook not only showcased his individual brilliance but also highlighted the ongoing duel between him and Larry Bird. This shot added yet another layer to their personal and team rivalry, with Magic stepping onto the Celtics' hallowed ground and delivering a moment that would be replayed in the annals of the NBA for generations.

Magic Johnson's baby skyhook became a defining moment in his career, symbolizing his ingenuity and clutch performance under pressure. It encapsulated the essence of the Showtime Lakers—a team that combined athletic brilliance with theatrical flair, all under the direction of their charismatic leader.

In the years that have followed, Magic's skyhook in the 1987 Finals has become a touchstone for basketball greatness, a single play that represents the convergence of skill, poise, and the will to win. It remains a poignant reminder of Magic Johnson's legacy as a player who could rise to the occasion when the stakes were highest and deliver a performance that would resonate far beyond the final buzzer.

The Shot Heard Around the World: Duke vs. Kentucky, 1992 NCAA Tournament

The East Regional Final of the 1992 NCAA Tournament was a collision of basketball titans, pitting the defending champions, the Duke Blue Devils, against a gritty Kentucky Wildcats team. The game itself was a back-and-forth affair, a true heavyweight bout that saw neither team able to deliver the knockout blow, leading to an overtime period that only heightened the already palpable tension in Philadelphia's Spectrum arena.

The overtime session was a microcosm of the game's intensity, featuring lead changes, strategic maneuvers, and individual heroics. The stage was set for a dramatic conclusion when Kentucky, behind a miraculous three-pointer by Sean Woods, took a one-point lead with just seconds remaining on the clock. Duke, facing the prospect of their championship reign ending, called a timeout to set up what would be one of the most iconic plays in sports history.

With 2.1 seconds left, the stage was set for a final play that would etch itself into the collective memory of basketball fans forever. Grant Hill, Duke's freshman forward, stood on the baseline tasked with the seemingly impossible job of delivering a full-court pass. On the receiving end was Christian Laettner, Duke's All-American, positioned at the opposite free-throw line surrounded by Kentucky defenders.

As Hill's pass sailed down the court, Laettner caught the ball with his back to the basket, took a single dribble, pivoted, and released a high-arcing jump shot. The ball sailed through the air as the buzzer sounded, and as it fell through the net, pandemonium ensued. Duke had snatched victory from the jaws of defeat.

The impact of "The Shot" was immediate and far-reaching. It propelled Duke to the Final Four and eventually to another NCAA title, cementing their status as a college basketball dynasty. For Kentucky, it was a heartbreaking end to an otherwise storybook run through the tournament, a defeat that would linger but also serve as a motivator for future success.

Laettner's perfect game—he was 10-for-10 from the field and 10-for-10 from the free-throw line—was crowned by his final shot, a moment that has been replayed countless times in March Madness montages. It stands as a testament to the pressure-cooker environment of the NCAA Tournament, where legends are made in the blink of an eye.

The Shot Heard Around the World transcended college basketball, becoming a cultural touchstone. It embodies the drama and excitement of March Madness, capturing the essence of what makes the tournament a national obsession. Christian Laettner's name became synonymous with clutch performance, and the game itself a reference point for basketball brilliance.

In the years since, the Duke-Kentucky clash has taken on a mythical quality, a game that is discussed with reverence and serves as a benchmark for what college basketball can offer in terms of excitement and athletic excellence. It was a game that had everything— star power, high stakes, and a conclusion that seems almost scripted for its perfect execution and dramatic flair.

The 1992 East Regional Final remains a pinnacle of college basketball history, a game that defines the unpredictability and allure of the NCAA Tournament. The Shot Heard Around the World endures as a moment that encapsulates the very heart of the sport—a heart that beats loudest when the pressure is highest, and the stage is set for heroes to emerge.

Reggie Miller's 8 Points in 9 Seconds: 1995 Eastern Conference Semifinals

The hallowed ground of Madison Square Garden set the stage for one of the most improbable comebacks in NBA playoff history. The New York Knicks, with a seemingly secure lead and the clock winding down, were poised to take a 1-0 series lead over the Indiana Pacers. The fans were already celebrating, the players' minds possibly already in the locker room. But Reggie Miller, the Pacers' sharpshooting guard, had other plans.

With just 18.7 seconds left on the clock and the Pacers trailing by six, the situation looked bleak for the visitors. What happened next would become a defining moment in NBA lore. Miller scored a quick three-pointer, stole the inbound pass, dribbled out beyond the arc, turned, and sank another three—all in the blink of an eye. The Garden was stunned into silence. Miller capped off his stunning performance by drawing a foul and sinking two free throws, completing an eight-point run that snatched victory from the jaws of defeat.

This moment was more than just a dramatic scoring burst; it was a chapter in the fierce rivalry between the Pacers and the Knicks. Miller's heroics amplified his status as a Knicks nemesis, a role he seemed to relish as much as the Garden crowd loathed him for it. The sight of Miller giving the choke sign and jawing with famed Knicks fan Spike Lee added a delicious subplot to the drama unfolding on the court.

Miller's performance was as much psychological warfare as it was a display of basketball prowess. His ability to get into the heads of the Knicks' players and fans alike showcased the intangible aspects of basketball—where confidence and the ability to intimidate can be as decisive as pure skill.

The game elevated Miller's reputation as one of the most clutch performers in NBA history. It wasn't just the points he scored, but when he scored them that mattered. Miller's legacy was built on moments like this—where his sharpshooting and fearlessness under pressure led to spectacular results.

Miller's 8 points in 9 seconds have become a yardstick for what it means to never give up, to always believe in the possibility of victory, no matter how distant it seems. It's a sequence that aspiring basketball players have watched and rewatched, drawing inspiration from Miller's calm under pressure and his lethal accuracy from beyond the three-point line.

Reggie Miller's miraculous finish against the Knicks is a testament to the power of belief, precision, and the ability to seize the moment. It's a reminder of why basketball fans remain glued to their seats until the final buzzer sounds because in those waning seconds, anything is possible. Miller's 8 points in 9 seconds remain a touchstone moment in NBA history, encapsulating the thrill of the game and the sheer unpredictability of playoff basketball.

Jordan's Flu Game: 1997 NBA Finals

On the eve of Game 5, with the series tied at two games apiece, the Chicago Bulls faced not only the formidable Utah Jazz but the uncertainty surrounding the condition of their leader, Michael Jordan. Struck by flu-like symptoms caused by food poisoning, Jordan's status was in doubt right up until tip-off. What unfolded that night at the Delta Center in Salt Lake City was nothing short of legendary.

From the opening minutes, it was clear that Jordan was far from his physical best. Pale and lethargic, he struggled to muster his usual explosiveness. Yet, as the game progressed, his resolve seemed only to strengthen. In what would become a defining image of his career, Jordan, exhausted and dehydrated, refused to yield, playing through his sickness with a determination that seemed to transcend the sport itself.

Jordan's heroics manifested in a 38-point tour de force that included seven rebounds, five assists, three steals, and the game-deciding three-pointer with just 25 seconds left on the clock. His ability to dominate while in such a weakened state spoke to his mental fortitude and competitive spirit—attributes that have become as synonymous with his legacy as his athletic prowess.

Adding to the mystique of the Flu Game is the pair of black and red Air Jordan 12s that he wore. These sneakers have since become emblematic of the game and are a tangible piece of NBA lore, representing the grit and grace Jordan exhibited on the court that night.

The significance of Jordan's performance transcended the stat sheet; it was an inspirational display that echoed the ethos of basketball and sport in general—the will to win against all odds. It was a testament to Jordan's sheer will and the psychological edge that he maintained over his opponents, even when physically compromised.

The Bulls' victory in Game 5 shifted the momentum of the series, setting the stage for their fifth NBA Championship in seven years. Jordan's "Flu Game" is often cited as the epitome of his career, a microcosm of his ability to rise to the occasion when the stakes were highest, and his tank was at its lowest.

The Flu Game stands as one of Michael Jordan's many career highlights, but perhaps none other encapsulates his indomitable spirit quite as poignantly. It is a reminder of human vulnerability and the potential for greatness that lies in the will to overcome. It is a chapter in the story of a man who was not only physically gifted but possessed an unyielding desire to triumph, no matter the circumstances.

Jordan's Flu Game is etched into basketball history not merely as a record of points scored but as a narrative of resilience and heart. It has become a benchmark against which other great performances are measured, a heroic feat that serves as inspiration for players at all levels of the sport. The Flu Game encapsulates the essence of Michael Jordan's greatness—a combination of skill, tenacity, and an unparalleled competitive drive that defined his illustrious career.

The Unbreakable Will: Kobe Bryant's 60-Point Farewell

April 13, 2016, marked the end of an era as Kobe Bryant, one of the greatest basketball players of all time, laced up for his final contest in a Los Angeles Lakers uniform. The Staples Center was electric, filled with an air of anticipation and nostalgia, as fans gathered to witness the final chapter of Kobe's 20-year saga with the Lakers.

The game was as much a celebration as it was a competition, with tributes pouring in from former teammates, rivals, and legends of the game. The atmosphere was one of collective gratitude for the two decades of memories Kobe had provided, and anticipation for one last display of his storied ability to captivate and amaze.

As the game against the Utah Jazz unfolded, it became clear that Kobe was not going to quietly fade away. Instead, he dominated the ball and the game, taking shots with the same ferocity and determination that had defined his career. His performance was a throwback to the days when he was the young phenom who would take over games with his scoring prowess.

Shot after shot, Kobe's point total climbed, harkening back to the days when he was the most feared scorer in the league. The 60 points he amassed were not just a testament to his skill but a manifestation of his character—his competitiveness, his refusal to settle, and his desire to leave an indelible mark on the game he loved.

Kobe's final points came from the free-throw line, a fitting conclusion for a player who had spent countless hours perfecting his craft. With each shot, the crowd rose in a crescendo of cheers, culminating in a standing ovation as he reached the 60-point milestone. The game ended with a victory for the Lakers, but the score was secondary to the spectacle of Kobe's final bow.

In his parting words, Kobe addressed the crowd with a simple, heartfelt "Mamba out," dropping the microphone and exiting the stage for the last time. The outpouring of emotion from fans, teammates, and even opponents spoke volumes about the impact of his career. It was a night that transcended sport, as fans around the world witnessed the close of one of basketball's greatest narratives.

Kobe's 60-point farewell was more than just an incredible athletic performance; it was a testament to the unbreakable will of one of the game's most iconic figures. It encapsulated the essence of Kobe's persona—the Mamba Mentality—that combination of talent, hard work, and psychological edge that made him a legend.

The story of Kobe Bryant's 60-point finale will be retold for generations, a legendary ending to a legendary career. It stands as a beacon of what it means to love and dedicate oneself to a craft, to compete with every fiber of one's being, and to exit not with a whimper, but with a roar. Kobe's final game was a microcosm of his career, a narrative woven from his first game to his last—a tale of passion, greatness, and an unbreakable will that inspired millions.

The Block, The Shot, The Championship: 2016 NBA Finals Game 7

June 19, 2016, was a day of reckoning in the world of basketball. The Cleveland Cavaliers and the Golden State Warriors, two teams at the pinnacle of the sport, converged on the Oracle Arena for the climax of a series that had already become a classic. The Warriors, coming off a record-breaking 73-win season, were pitted against a Cavaliers team seeking to end a 52-year championship drought for the city of Cleveland.

The game was a rollercoaster from the start, an intense back-and-forth between two well-matched adversaries. The Warriors' sharpshooting duo of Stephen Curry and Klay Thompson traded blows with the Cavaliers' LeBron James and Kyrie Irving in a game that was as much a mental battle as it was physical. With each quarter, the lead changed, the momentum shifted, and the tension built.

With less than two minutes to go and the game tied, the Warriors' Andre Iguodala broke away for what seemed like a sure layup, only for LeBron James to make a chase-down block of epic proportions. "The Block" was a moment of pure athleticism and willpower, a defensive play that shifted the destiny of the game and became one of the most iconic moments in NBA history.

Not long after, with the game still knotted up and under a minute left, Kyrie Irving stepped up to etch his name into basketball lore. Irving's three-pointer over Curry was a shot of audacity and poise, a dagger that pierced the heart of the Oracle Arena and the Warriors' hopes.

The final buzzer heralded a victory for the Cavaliers, but the echoes of that game resonated far beyond the court. LeBron James's promise to bring a championship to his home state had been realized, and the image of him collapsing on the floor, overcome with emotion, symbolized the relief and joy of an entire city.

This Game 7 was about more than just a title; it was a narrative of redemption, resilience, and the rewriting of history. It was the first time a team had come back from a 3-1 deficit in the NBA Finals, a testament to the Cavaliers' unyielding spirit and the incredible journey they had undertaken.

The legacy of this game extends into the cultural fabric, a reminder of the power of sports to unite and uplift. It encapsulated the essence of competition, the drama of high-stakes basketball, and the personal narratives of the players involved, particularly LeBron James, whose journey from prodigy to pariah and back to champion is a tale of redemption and determination.

The Block, The Shot, and The Championship of the 2016 NBA Finals Game 7 have become part of basketball's collective consciousness. It was a game that defined careers, fulfilled promises, and transformed the legacy of a city and its star player. In the annals of the NBA, it will forever stand as a game that was about more than the final score, a game that captured the very soul of basketball and its capacity to inspire awe and wonder.

Chapter 9:
The Culture of Basketball: Movies, Books, and Fashion

asketball transcends the boundaries of a mere sport to influence and be influenced by broader cultural realms. This chapter explores how basketball has permeated various aspects of culture, including cinema, literature, and fashion, reflecting its significance beyond the court.

Basketball in Cinema: Capturing the Essence of the Game

Basketball's journey in the world of cinema has been one of evocative storytelling and cultural reflection. Films centered around basketball have ranged from inspiring sports dramas to comedies, each weaving the essence of the game into narratives that speak to a wide range of audiences.

"Hoosiers," based on a true story, is a classic underdog tale that transcends basketball. It captures the essence of small-town America's love for the sport, highlighting themes like teamwork, perseverance, and the unlikely triumph of an underdog. The film's portrayal of a high school team's journey to the state championship is a poignant reminder of how sports can unite communities and inspire individuals.

"White Men Can't Jump" is another seminal basketball movie that blends humor with social commentary. It explores the dynamic world of street basketball, delving into themes of race, friendship, and the hustle of survival. The film's witty dialogue and the chemistry between its leads brought a different, more light-hearted perspective to basketball's representation in cinema.

"Space Jam" took basketball to a fantastical dimension, combining the sport with beloved Looney Tunes characters. It introduced the game to younger audiences, immortalizing Michael Jordan's legacy in a fun and imaginative way. The film's blend of animation and live-action was not only an entertainment feat but also a symbol of basketball's expansive cultural influence.

Documentaries like "Hoop Dreams" offer a stark contrast to fictionalized portrayals, providing a more realistic and often grittier view of the sport. Following the lives of two aspiring basketball players from inner-city Chicago, "Hoop Dreams" showcases the challenges and hopes tied to basketball as a pathway to a better life. It's a powerful exploration of the American dream as seen through the lens of young athletes.

"The Last Dance," a more recent documentary, captivated audiences with its in-depth look at the Chicago Bulls' dynasty through the lens of Michael Jordan's career. It offered unparalleled insights into

Jordan's character, the intensity of professional sports, and the complexities of team dynamics.

Other films have used basketball as a backdrop to explore personal struggles and societal issues. Movies like "Love & Basketball" intertwine the pursuit of professional athletic careers with themes of love, gender, and personal growth. They depict the sport as a metaphor for life's challenges and triumphs.

Basketball movies and documentaries have done more than just depict the sport on screen; they have contributed to the cultural narrative surrounding basketball. They provide a window into different aspects of the game, from the high-stakes world of professional play to the raw passion found on street courts. These films often resonate with viewers because they reflect broader human experiences - of striving for greatness, facing adversity, and the pursuit of dreams.

Basketball's representation in cinema has been varied and impactful, offering both entertainment and profound insights into the sport. These films and documentaries have played a significant role in popularizing basketball, influencing public perception, and showcasing the game's deeper societal and cultural connections. Through the lens of cinema, basketball is celebrated not just as a game, but as a compelling narrative of human experience.

Literature: Chronicling Basketball's Impact

The world of literature has embraced basketball, offering a diverse range of works that explore the sport from multiple perspectives. These works range from detailed analyses and historical accounts to deeply personal memoirs and imaginative fiction, each adding depth and understanding to the cultural significance of basketball.

Books like "The Book of Basketball" by Bill Simmons offer comprehensive overviews, delving into the history of the NBA and offering a blend of statistical analysis, humorous anecdotes, and insightful commentary. Such works often provide readers with a deeper appreciation of the sport, its evolution, and the personalities that have shaped it.

Phil Jackson's "Eleven Rings" is another seminal work, offering insights into the strategies and philosophies of one of basketball's most successful coaches. Jackson's exploration of leadership and team dynamics provides valuable lessons that extend beyond the basketball court.

Autobiographies and memoirs of basketball figures offer intimate glimpses into the lives and minds of those who have left their mark on the sport. "The Mamba Mentality" by Kobe Bryant is more than just a recounting of a storied career; it's an exploration of the dedication and mental approach that drove one of basketball's greatest players.

Other works like "When the Game Was Ours" by Larry Bird and Magic Johnson with Jackie MacMullan provide a dual narrative of the rivalry and friendship between two of the game's legends, offering readers a unique perspective on the moments that defined an era of basketball.

Basketball-themed literature also delves into the sport's intersection with societal and personal issues. "The Basketball Diaries" by Jim Carroll is a stark, moving memoir that chronicles the author's teenage years, where basketball and a descent into drug addiction coexist, reflecting the sport's role in the broader narrative of his life.

John Edgar Wideman's "Hoops" and Walter Dean Myers' "Slam!" are examples of fiction that use basketball as a backdrop to explore themes such as identity, race, and the challenges of inner-city life. These stories resonate with readers for their authentic portrayal of the struggles and triumphs associated with the sport.

Basketball literature also includes inspirational and educational titles aimed at younger audiences. These works often combine the excitement of the game with lessons on teamwork, perseverance, and achieving one's dreams. They are instrumental in introducing the sport to new generations and instilling a love for the game.

Here are two notable examples: "Salt in His Shoes: Michael Jordan in Pursuit of a Dream" by Deloris Jordan with Roslyn M. Jordan. This children's book, written by Michael Jordan's mother and sister, tells the inspirational story of a young Michael Jordan, who dreams of becoming a great basketball player. The story focuses on the themes of patience, determination, and hard work. It narrates how young Michael, with the support of his family, overcomes obstacles and doubts about his height and abilities. Illustrated with charming artwork, the book is not only about basketball but also about growing up and the value of perseverance.

"The Crossover" is a novel written in verse that captures the energy and rhythm of basketball while telling a heartfelt story. The book focuses on 12-year-old twin basketball stars, Josh and Jordan (JB) Bell, who encounter challenges on and off the court. This Newbery Medal-winning book beautifully weaves together themes of family, brotherhood, and coming-of-age, all set against the backdrop of the basketball court. Its engaging, rhythmic prose makes it an appealing read for young readers, effectively conveying the excitement of basketball while imparting important life lessons.

Literature has played a significant role in chronicling the impact of basketball, offering a rich and varied exploration of the game and its cultural significance. These works have served to deepen our understanding and appreciation of basketball, not only as a sport but as a phenomenon that intersects with and reflects broader societal narratives and personal journeys.

Fashion: The Intersection of Basketball and Style

The fusion of basketball and fashion represents more than a mere overlap of interests; it's a cultural phenomenon that has shaped and redefined style trends. Basketball's influence on fashion is evident in various aspects, from footwear to apparel, and has evolved to become a significant part of the sport's cultural identity.

At the forefront of this intersection is the sneaker culture, largely propelled by basketball. Iconic shoes like the Air Jordans, first introduced by Nike with Michael Jordan, have become much more than athletic wear. They sparked a sneaker revolution, becoming coveted items for collectors and fashion enthusiasts alike. These sneakers represent a blend of performance design and aesthetic appeal, often associated with the charisma and achievements of the players they are named after.

Other basketball shoes, like the Adidas Superstar and Converse Chuck Taylor All-Stars, have also transcended their court origins to become staples in casual fashion. Their widespread adoption by musicians, actors, and other celebrities has further cemented their status in popular culture.

Modern basketball players have become fashion icons in their own right. Stars like Russell Westbrook, LeBron James, and James Harden are known for their distinctive and often avant-garde fashion choices. Their pre-game entrances and post-game press conferences have become runways, showcasing personal styles that range from elegantly tailored suits to cutting-edge streetwear.

These players have also collaborated with fashion brands and designers, creating their own clothing lines or sneaker designs. Their influence extends beyond the basketball fan base, impacting broader fashion trends and often making statements about identity and culture.

The relationship between basketball and fashion has led to an interesting integration of high fashion with streetwear. Luxury brands have tapped into basketball's popularity, creating collections that draw inspiration from the sport's aesthetic and cultural impact. This has resulted in unique collaborations where the grit and dynamism of basketball are fused with the sophistication of high fashion.

Basketball's influence in fashion also extends to general apparel. While team jerseys have always been popular among fans, there's been a growing trend of basketball-inspired clothing. This includes graphic tees, hoodies, and shorts that incorporate basketball themes, team logos, and player images, crafted to be stylish and comfortable, suitable for both the court and everyday wear.

For many players and fans, basketball fashion has become a medium for personal and political expression. Athletes often use their attire to make statements on social issues, support causes, or express their cultural backgrounds. This aspect of basketball fashion highlights its role not just in style, but in personal identity and social commentary.

The fusion of basketball and fashion is dynamic and influential, reflecting the sport's cultural significance. It's a realm where athleticism meets aesthetics, where the styles and trends are constantly evolving. This intersection has not only enriched the world of fashion but also added a vibrant dimension to the culture of basketball, illustrating how the sport extends its influence far beyond the boundaries of the court.

The Influence of Hip-Hop Culture

The relationship between basketball and hip-hop culture is deep and symbiotic, with each having a profound influence on the other. This cultural fusion has roots in the urban landscapes of America, where both basketball and hip-hop emerged as powerful forms of expression among youth, particularly in African American communities.

The influence of hip-hop in basketball is palpable in the ambiance of the arenas. Hip-hop music has become a staple in pre-game, in-game, and post-game festivities. The energetic beats and rhythms of hip-hop tracks not only entertain the crowd but also energize the players, often serving as pump-up anthems that resonate with both the athletes and the audience.

Hip-hop culture has significantly influenced the fashion sense of basketball players. The style typically associated with hip-hop — baggy shorts, oversized jerseys, sneakers, and an overall relaxed, street-savvy look — became popular among basketball players, both on and off the court. This style was in stark contrast to the more traditional, conservative dress codes that were once prevalent in the sport, leading to a more expressive and relatable image for the players.

Basketball has been a recurring theme in hip-hop music and videos, with numerous songs referencing basketball players, teams, and the sport itself. These references have not only helped popularize the sport but have also solidified the cultural connection between basketball and hip-hop. Music videos featuring basketball themes or cameos by players further reinforce this connection, blurring the lines between sports and music entertainment.

The cross-influence of basketball and hip-hop extends to language and communication styles. Slang and terminologies from basketball have made their way into hip-hop lyrics, and vice versa. This shared language has contributed to a unique lexicon that is recognizable and widely used among fans of both basketball and hip-hop.

Basketball players often cite hip-hop artists as influences and role models, and many hip-hop artists are avid basketball fans, frequently spotted at games. This mutual admiration has led to collaborations and partnerships that transcend music and sports, creating cultural icons who have a significant impact on youth and popular culture.

Both basketball and hip-hop have played roles in community development and social activism. They provide platforms for discussing social issues, fostering community engagement, and promoting positive change. Many basketball players and hip-hop artists use their influence to inspire and uplift communities, leveraging their popularity for philanthropic efforts.

The integration of basketball and hip-hop culture represents more than just a mutual appreciation between two popular forms of entertainment. It is a dynamic convergence that has shaped the cultural landscape, influencing fashion, language, music, and social attitudes. This fusion has not only enhanced the appeal and reach of both basketball and hip-hop but has also played a significant role in cultural expression and identity formation, particularly among younger generations.

The Role of Video Games and Digital Media

The digital realm, particularly video games and digital media, has significantly expanded basketball's reach and influence. Titles like the NBA 2K series have become more than just a form of entertainment; they serve as interactive platforms that deepen fans' connection to the sport.

Modern basketball video games offer an unprecedented level of realism and immersion. They meticulously replicate player likenesses, team strategies, and even the atmosphere of real-world arenas. Fans can experience the thrill of playing as their favorite athletes, understanding their skills and styles in a way that was not possible before. This level of detail extends to replicating players' moves, team playbooks, and even the commentary, making the gaming experience incredibly authentic.

For many fans, basketball video games are a tool for learning and understanding the sport. By playing these games, fans can gain a deeper appreciation of basketball strategies, player roles, and game rules. This interactive form of learning is particularly appealing to younger audiences, who often use these games as a gateway to becoming basketball fans.

The rise of eSports has brought a competitive edge to basketball video games. Online tournaments and leagues mirror the structure of real basketball leagues, with players and teams competing for championships. This aspect of digital basketball has its own fan base, with skilled gamers gaining fame and following in the eSports community.

Video games have also facilitated the formation of online communities where fans can connect, discuss, and share their love for basketball. These communities are platforms for fans to engage in discussions, share gameplay tips, and even organize virtual matches. In this way, basketball video games have fostered a sense of community and belonging among fans worldwide.

From a marketing perspective, basketball video games are a powerful tool for player engagement and brand promotion. They provide an additional platform for teams and players to connect with fans, particularly the younger demographic. In-game advertising, player endorsements, and special game events linked to real-world basketball are ways in which the sport's marketing potential is realized in the digital realm.

Basketball video games have also influenced popular culture, with references to these games appearing in music, movies, and other media. They contribute to the mainstream visibility of the sport and its athletes, further embedding basketball in the cultural consciousness.

The role of video games and digital media in basketball represents a significant shift in how fans interact with the sport. These platforms offer immersive, interactive experiences that enhance fans' understanding and enjoyment of basketball. As technology continues to advance, the potential for even more innovative and engaging digital basketball experiences seems boundless, ensuring that the sport remains relevant and appealing in the digital age.

In conclusion, basketball's impact on movies, books, and fashion underscores its status as a cultural phenomenon. It's a sport that captures the imagination, inspires creativity, and resonates with people across various walks of life. As basketball continues to evolve, so too does its cultural footprint, enriching and being enriched by the diverse domains it touches.

Chapter 10:
Just for Fun: Basketball Trivia

eyond the intense matchups and buzzer-beaters lies a lighter
and equally engaging aspect of basketball – trivia. This
chapter is a celebration of the fun and fascinating facts
surrounding the game, designed to challenge and entertain basketball
fans of all levels with intriguing questions about the sport's history,
legends, and quirky details. So, get off the bench, jump into the game
and see how many of your answers are nothing but net! The answers
to the questions can be found at the end of the chapter.

Questions

1. Who invented basketball and in what year?

2. Which team won the first-ever NBA Championship?

3. Who has the record for the most points scored in a single
   NBA game?

4. What team did Michael Jordan play for in his NBA debut?

5. Which player has won the most NBA MVP awards?

6. Who is the shortest player to ever play in the NBA?

7. What is the diameter of a standard NBA basketball hoop?

8. Which NBA team holds the record for the longest winning streak in a single season?

9. What player was known as "The Round Mound of Rebound"?

10. Who was the first player to be drafted in the first-ever NBA Draft in 1947?

11. Which player has the most career assists in the NBA?

12. What female player was the first to dunk in a WNBA game?

13. Who holds the record for the most points scored in an NBA playoff game?

14. Which country outside the USA has produced the most NBA players?

15. Which NBA player starred in the movie "Space Jam"?

16. What is the regulation height of an NBA basketball hoop?

17. Who is the youngest player to score 10,000 points in the NBA?

18. What NBA team did Magic Johnson play his entire career for?

19. Who was the first woman to coach in the NBA?

20. How many teams are there in the NBA?

21. What player has won the most NBA championships as a player?

22. Who was the first European player to win the NBA MVP award?

23. What year was the three-point line introduced in the NBA?

24. Who was the first high school player to be drafted first overall in the NBA Draft?

25. Which NBA team did Kobe Bryant score his highest career points (81 points) against?

Answers

1. Dr. James Naismith in 1891

2. The Philadelphia Warriors in 1947

3. Wilt Chamberlain, with 100 points

4. The Chicago Bulls

5. Kareem Abdul-Jabbar, with six MVP awards

6. Tyrone "Muggsy" Bogues, who stood 5 feet 3 inches tall

7. 18 inches

8. The Los Angeles Lakers, with 33 wins in the 1971-72 season

9. Charles Barkley

10. Clifton McNeely by the Pittsburgh Ironmen

11. John Stockton with 15,806 assists

12. Lisa Leslie in 2002

13. Michael Jordan, with 63 points in Game 2 of the 1986 First Round against the Celtics

14. Canada

15. Michael Jordan

16. 10 feet

17. LeBron James: 23 years, 59 days

18. The Los Angeles Lakers

19. Becky Hammon as an assistant coach for the San Antonio Spurs

20. 30 teams

21. Bill Russell, with 11 championships

22. Dirk Nowitzki

23. 1979

24. Kwame Brown in 2001

25. The Toronto Raptors in 2006

Chapter 11:
Final Reflections: The Heart of Basketball

In summarizing the essence of basketball, we find a sport that transcends the physical boundaries of courts and arenas. It is a journey that mirrors life itself, filled with highs and lows, challenges and triumphs, and moments of individual brilliance harmonizing with team synergy. Basketball teaches lessons that extend far beyond winning games; it imparts wisdom about perseverance, collaboration, and the pursuit of excellence.

Basketball emerges as a profound teacher, imparting lessons not easily found in textbooks. It teaches the value of discipline and hard work, the importance of teamwork and unity, and the strength found in diversity and inclusivity. On the court, players learn about responsibility, leadership, and the significance of playing a role for the greater good.

The unifying force of basketball is remarkable. It has the power to bring together people from different walks of life, creating a common language understood by all who play, watch, or engage with it. In times of division, basketball has often served as a bridge, bringing communities together and fostering a sense of belonging and togetherness.

Basketball's influence on communities is undeniable. From urban neighborhoods to rural areas, from local gyms to international arenas, it has the power to uplift, empower, and transform. Basketball courts have become community centers, places where young people find guidance, where talent is nurtured, and where lifelong friendships are forged.

The sport has also played a significant role in breaking down cultural barriers. It has brought global attention to various issues, celebrated cultural diversity, and contributed to international understanding and respect. Through basketball, people have learned about different cultures, traditions, and perspectives, enriching their own lives in the process.

The legacy of basketball is not just in the records set or the championships won, but in the lives it has touched and the positive changes it has brought about. It's a legacy of inspiring individuals to reach their potential, of building resilient communities, and of creating a more inclusive world.

As we conclude this exploration of basketball, it's clear that the sport is about much more than the physical act of shooting a ball through a hoop. It's about the joy it brings, the lives it shapes, and the communities it builds. Basketball is a celebration of human potential, a testament to the power of unity, and a beacon of hope and inspiration. Its true essence lies in its ability to connect us, challenge us, and elevate us. In the end, basketball is indeed more than just a game - it's a profound and enduring part of the human experience.

Made in the USA
Monee, IL
12 March 2024

54884225R00075